Ecologism

MICHAEL J. HEVERIN

Concepts in the Social Sciences

Series Editor: Frank Parkin

Published Titles

Democracy (Second Edition)	*Anthony Arblaster*
Discrimination	*Michael Banton*
Citizenship	*J. M. Barbalet*
Welfare	*Norman Barry*
Freedom	*Zygmunt Bauman*
Bureaucracy (Second Edition)	*David Beetham*
Nationalism	*Craig Calhoun*
Trotskyism	*Alex Callinicos*
Revolution and Counter-Revolution	*Peter Calvert*
Policy	*H. K. Colebatch*
Socialism	*Bernard Crick*
Exchange	*John Davis*
Social Science	*Gerard Delanty*
Power	*Keith Dowding*
Rights	*Michael Freeden*
Science	*Steve Fuller*
Liberalism (Second Edition)	*John Gray*
The State	*John A. Hall and G. John Ikenberry*
Kinship	*C. C. Harris*
Utopianism	*Krishan Kumar*
Postmodernity	*David Lyon*
Ideology (Second Edition)	*David McLellan*
Pluralism	*Gregor McLennan*
Fascism	*Mark Neocleous*
Conservatism	*Robert Nisbet*
Race and Ethnicity	*John Rex*
Capitalism	*Peter Saunders*
Class	*Richard Scase*
Ecologism	*Mark J. Smith*
Status	*Bryan S. Turner*

Concepts in the Social Sciences

Ecologism

Towards Ecological Citizenship

Mark J. Smith

Open University Press
Buckingham

Open University Press
Celtic Court
22 Ballmoor
Buckingham
MK18 1XW

email: enquiries@openup.co.uk
world wide web: http://www.openup.co.uk

First published 1998

A catalogue record of this book is available from the British Library

ISBN 0 335 19604 7 (hb) 0 335 19603 9 (pb)

Typeset by Type Study, Scarborough
Printed in Great Britain by St Edmundsbury Press, Bury St Edmunds, Suffolk

For Gemma

Contents

Acknowledgements

I am grateful to many people for their help and support while this text was being written. In particular, thanks are due to Mark Neocleous for suggesting the idea of the book in the first place and to Christine Meeks for her careful secretarial work on the manuscript. I should like to acknowledge the patience, encouragement and support of Frank Parkin (the editor of the series), Gaynor Clements and Justin Vaughan at Open University Press. I am also grateful to the students who attended my courses on ecology at the University of Sussex for many lively discussions, as well as to William Outhwaite, Luke Martell and Peter Dickens for intellectual inspiration. Most of all, thank you to Jane, Harry and George.

1 Introduction: Understanding Nature

The end of one century and the start of a new one offers a moment's pause for reflection on the assumptions and values which we hold to be important. These brief historical conjunctures at the close of centuries are often referred to as *fin de siècle* periods, to mark their status as periods of doubt and reassessment. At the end of the twentieth century and the start of the twenty-first, one issue seems to fascinate us more than any other: the relationship between society and nature. In short, we are fascinated with the green environment and what it means to our social existence. In modern societies, since the sixteenth century, one way of thinking through this relationship has predominated: the anthropocentric or human-centred approach. This dominant conception of how the environment is understood and valued has many variations but, at its core, there is the desire to ensure human mastery over the natural world and that natural things exist for the use and welfare of human beings. This book attempts to demonstrate how and why this underlying idea has come to be questioned and what this means for rethinking the relationship between society and nature. More than this, I will argue that such questions have prompted a new phase in thinking about the green environment. This new way of thinking is based upon a set of assumptions which displace human beings from the central position they have occupied in social and political evaluation. This is a position I define as *ecologism*.

The word 'ecology' is ancient in origin, derived from the Greek term *oikos*, from which the word 'economy' was also derived. The earliest recorded use of the term 'economy of nature' can be identified in the naturalist writings of Kenelm Digby in 1658; the same term was used in the title of the foundational botanical text by Linnaeus in 1749. This association of ecology with natural processes, rather than with human ones, was to continue through the writings of Alexander von Humboldt, on the balance and harmony of nature, as well as in Charles Darwin's account of the evolution of different species. Darwin's analysis of the origin of the human species, in particular its stress on the common biological heritage with primates, was a crucial step in undermining the sense of privilege which underpins the idea of human mastery over nature. At the same time, Ernst Haeckel coined the term 'ecology' to designate a definite field of human knowledge which could claim the title 'science'. Haeckel also established the idea that all species, including humans, were part of a complex and changing set of relationships. It should be emphasized that many ecological studies took place with the central aim of ensuring a more effective human mastery over nature, rather than any sense of living in harmony with the ecosystem.

Our concern, in this text, is with the green environment, the place of human beings within it and what it means to us. The green environment includes humans, animals, insects, fishes, plants, rocks, trees, waterfalls, rivers, oceans, mountains and the ecosystem or biosphere. The expression 'natural environment' is often used as a descriptive label for non-human processes, whereas the 'green environment' enables us to think of natural things and their interrelationships with human beings. For reasons of brevity, I will generally ignore the built environment, the urban environment and the social environment, except in so far as they have an impact upon how we interpret the natural environment. Rather than considering social ecology, which involves the study of how social organizations work, we will consider the meanings human beings construct about natural ecology. More specifically, we will explore the ways in which the value of ecological systems has changed and is changing again today. Scientific ecology tended to focus almost exclusively on the biological processes and relationships between different organisms in a variety of natural habitats. For much of its existence, ecology referred either purely to social organization or solely to natural relations. The meaning of the word 'ecology' now seems to have broadened, so that the activities of the human species have to be taken into account as part of these processes and relationships. This is partly because human beings have radically altered the environment and partly because scientists are responding to an increase in awareness of the impact of human beings upon nature.

In short, we will focus upon the 'ways of seeing' the environment. When we describe and categorize what we observe, we also make judgements. There is no simple or neutral act of perception, for we see natural things as having a value and a status. When we give things a label, we also give them a standing, a position in a pecking order, an estimate of moral worth. For example, the distinction between 'man' and 'beast' is full of evocative meanings and clearly attempts to separate human beings from animals even though we remain, of course, a peculiar form of animal. The word 'man' derives meaning from its negation of the word 'beast'. To be a beast is to be savage, to have no moral constraints (to be amoral) and to be guided by instinct. In turn, this means that to be a 'man' is to be civilized, to know and understand moral constraints, as well as to use rational thought as a basis for communication and action. In so doing, we place values on the things we talk about through the very words we use. In turn, these words only make sense within the systems of values we share within social communities. Every word we use to understand natural things is packed full of meaning and we need to tread carefully if we are to avoid some of these problems.

This book has two main themes. First, how do we value the environment? To address this issue we will briefly explore some of the most important ethical debates in human relations with the green environment, notably our obligations to future human generations and the considerations of non-human animals. Second, what implications do the debates over valuing the environment have for existing approaches towards justice, entitlements and obligations? To do this we will examine the impact of ecological thought upon definite traditions within social and political theory, namely liberalism, conservatism, socialism, feminism and anarchism. More than this, I will claim that the emergence of ecologism goes further than simply raising the possibility of greening these traditions. It also offers the opportunity for fundamentally rethinking the ground upon which these traditions stand. In short, ecological thought raises problems which are unlike any problems that human beings have ever faced before. Such radically new problems demand radically new solutions. Therefore, we need to think about them in innovative ways if we are to offer any hope of solving them. Before we tackle any of these substantive issues, it is important that we consider how our present ways of constructing and valuing the environment came about.

Anthropocentrism and ecocentrism

One key theme which runs throughout modern thinking about nature is anthropocentrism. This involves the foundational assumption that human beings, and the ways in which they value nature, are the *modus operandi* of any attempt to think about the green environment. Clearly, in order for human beings to understand the environment, the human imagination will always be involved. But does this mean that one part of the ecosystem, ourselves, should always be the measure of all things? Anthropocentric approaches assume that it does, that nature is only valuable in so far as human beings have a use for it. More than that, it is common to think of natural things as having a value only if human beings have transformed them into some useful product. Now, there is a clear difference between maintaining a forest for walking, picnics and other forms of recreation and chopping down the trees to make tables and chairs. However, there is something which both activities have in common. From the anthropocentric standpoint, this forest or these trees only have value because human beings value them for human purposes. If we follow through the implications of this approach, then, in a society in which there was no recreation, the value of the forest would be identified solely in terms of its conversion into an assortment of furniture. This approach is often regarded as an instrumental view of natural things, for they are seen as only having value in terms of human needs.

Anthropocentrism is also often associated with technocentrism, the belief that human beings are in a position, through the possession of scientific knowledge, to understand and control natural processes to such an extent that it is even possible to resolve all environmental problems by technological means. This is sometimes referred to as a 'technofix' approach. However, this obscures some vital differences between anthropocentrism and technocentrism. Perhaps the most important of these is that scientific thinking emerged as an attempt to remove anthropocentric assumptions from scientific knowledge. Some of the confusions over these differences are a product of the way in which scientific thinking has developed over the last two hundred years. Despite many attempts to define 'objective knowledge', in each case the criteria developed to distinguish scientific from non-scientific knowledge have been revealed to rest upon value-laden assumptions. Moreover, at the end of the day, modern scientific thinking has, at its core, the aim to develop human progress and benefit human material needs. Science was devised to conquer and master the forces of nature.

So, is there an alternative way of thinking about nature and values? Since this is a debate made by human beings for human beings, there is no escaping the problem of human values, for they inhabit every word which we use. Every description of natural things is full of meanings, many of which we can barely express for they act as the taken-for-granted assumptions upon which human beings act in the world. For instance, think about the ways in which natural things are described as machines, such as the planets operating like clockwork or chickens as machines for laying eggs. These analogies and metaphors are a crucial part of the process of constructing the meaning of natural things, for they make them tangible and immediate. The question, then, is not how we escape human valuation but whether it is possible to think of ways in which the value of natural things is not subordinate to the way they gratify the consumption patterns of human beings. If we are to look into the eye of anthropocentrism and challenge it, does this mean that human beings are no longer in control and that nature is in control instead? Is it possible to take the instrumental needs of the human species out of the central place in the value system, to displace human beings in the hierarchy of importance, and think of different ways of valuing things? It is to this alternative, the ecocentric approach, that we now turn.

Ecocentrism places human beings in a different relationship to the natural environment. The focus of ecocentrism is the ecosystem itself. This has been described in various ways as the biosphere, the network, the web, and so on, but what these descriptions all have in common is the focus on all living and life-supporting things and the interconnections between them. This means that human beings are part of a more complex system and no longer sit at the top of the ethical hierarchy (even if they still occupy the top of the food chain). The ecocentric approach raises questions about the anthropocentric approach by problematizing the boundaries and distinctions upon which it is based. For example, the idea that human beings have a privileged ethical standpoint makes little sense if it is not possible to identify fundamental differences between humans and natural things. This can be seen in the problems in identifying an absolute criterion for separating all human beings from all non-human animals. If no simple and clear criteria can be identified, then anthropocentrism is simply a prejudice.

Keith Thomas, in his mammoth study of the emergence and changing forms of anthropocentrism, *Man and the Natural World 1500–1800* (1982), provides a useful starting point for understanding these issues. Thomas reconstructs the ways in which the natural world has been understood in the early modern period. He argues that Christian biblical teachings served as the foundation for placing human beings at the centre of creation. According to the Christian view of the world, humans could consume animals just as animals consumed one another or consumed plants and insects. Human beings occupied the top of the food chain in a complex hierarchical natural order, which had been created through divine intervention. The food chain had become the basis of an ethical system in which human beings were clearly identified as superior to other forms of life. Within this world-view, all natural things had a purpose in the divine plan, either to feed, cloth, maintain or entertain human beings. The enhancement of human life lay at the centre of this ethical system. The superiority of human beings was justified, at one time or another, through their capacities for rational thought, political judgement and opinion, religious belief, the use of tools and scientific instruments, and even their capacity for laughter.

In the early modern period, René Descartes developed this underlying assumption of anthropocentrism within scientific thought by constructing the analogy that natural things could be seen as machines. Animals, it was argued, were simply complex machines with impulses and reflexes, for they were not equipped with the capacity for sensation, language, rational thought and suffering. For Thomas, this means that firm lines were drawn in the sand between humans and animals in order to justify hunting, domestication, vivisection and meat consumption, as well as mining and forest clearance. Thomas provides a historical sociology of human understandings of natural things. The focus is upon the role such views and values play in the cultures within which they operate. In particular, Thomas identifies the ways in which cultures tend to anthropomorphize natural things, that is, attribute social qualities to animals, weather systems and other natural things. This operates on a number of levels, ranging from expressions like 'as drunk as a dog' and 'as promiscuous as a rabbit' to more general analogies and metaphors such as the eponymous 'mother earth'. In short, it is possible to think of human regard for natural things as an index of morality. The Enlightenment thinker, Immanuel Kant, expressed this when he suggested that we should not treat animals badly because this was an indicator of how we treat other human beings.

The connections between anthropocentrism and Christianity are worth exploring in more detail, in order to demonstrate that Christian ethics does not provide a common line on the treatment of nature. So far, I have emphasized the 'nature is there to be exploited' approach. This has been identified, most notably, by Lynn White Junior (1967). White emphasizes the role of Judaeo-Christianity in establishing the separation of human beings and nature. In addition, she suggests, Judaeo-Christianity constructed the idea of the hierarchy of natural things with human beings as superior to all other parts in the chain of being (a theme which runs throughout the Old Testament from Genesis). The consequences of this conception of nature became more apparent in the ways in which it underpinned the Western value system. We can see something of this in the way in which John Locke defined property as anything with which human beings have mixed their labour provided that no other human beings have a prior claim. For Locke, property, alongside life and limb, was a God-given natural right. Within the industrializing societies of western Europe and North America, which have experienced massive and increasingly rapid technological transformations over the last 150 years, this value system regarded all natural things as open to exploitation for human gain. Only in industrial societies do we witness the capacity for immense ecological damage and the possibility of some form of ecological catastrophe.

The problem with White's account stems, in part, from the distinction used to characterize Judaeo-Christianity in opposition to Graeco-Christianity; the latter, has a greater respect for natural things. Actually, respect for nature can also be located in scriptures and historical sources in the Judaeo-Christian tradition as well.

From the book of Genesis through to the New Testament, the relationship between humans and nature can be interpreted as a tenancy rather than freehold ownership, as nurturing rather than exploitative, and as respectful rather than disrespectful. In this current within Christian ethics, the stewardship of nature is considered more appropriate than naked exploitation, so that God's creations became more abundant and luscious. The variety of conceptions of 'nature' in Christianity and in other religious belief systems (for Christianity is not alone in containing instrumental conceptions of nature) suggests that we should be more sensitive to the essentially contested character of the idea of nature. This is why the account of nature developed by Thomas is so important, for it identifies which conceptions of nature became relevant in the modern period in the Western world and helps us understand how these were translated into human impacts on the ecosystem.

Understanding nature in the modern world

There was, of course, considerable awareness of ecological damage before and during the industrialization process proper. The impact of the various processes which created the modern world, from the development of large-scale factory production and urbanization through to the emergence of a global market system, all transformed the natural environment. On the one hand, the environment provided natural resources which could be mixed with human labour in order to make property. The carbon deposits stored for millennia within the earth's crust served as an abundant source of fuel. On the other hand, the natural ecosystems provided an immense rubbish dump for human wastes and by-products which could not be put to good use. Up to a point, the ecosystems could absorb such impacts or adapt to such changes through modifications. For instance, it was often assumed that rivers could cleanse themselves of pollution over ten miles of their passage. However, when the population density reached a certain level and human productive activity intensified, the ecosystems were often damaged or fundamentally transformed. For instance, the forest and wood clearance in Britain pre-dates the industrial revolution and really accelerated during the early modern period, with the increase in demand for wood to be used for the construction of ships. Much of the land had already been turned over to farming so that the patchwork quilt of the English landscape was already well established as the natural landscape. This process was simply accelerated by the growing demands for agricultural produce from the emerging towns. The familiar patterns of the English landscape were already human-made.

It was, however, the impact of factory production, with its prodigious demands for more materials, more labour and more water, which was to solicit the most explicit attempts to highlight the negative impacts of the ever expanding growth of industry. Concern about the environment can be seen in the paintings of John Constable, the romantic poetry of Samuel Coleridge and William Wordsworth and the commentaries of John Ruskin. Both Wordsworth and the American writer, Henry David Thoreau, articulated a new sensibility based upon the aesthetic appreciation of the natural environment and the need for human beings to live in some form of holistic relationship with nature. For these artists and writers, rather than natural things being there to exploit at our whim, human beings occupied a small part of a much larger and complex system of relationships. In particular, they emphasized the ways in which small-scale household industry and smallhold farming drew from but did not disturb the natural order. But how natural was this order? The Lake District landscape was already significantly transformed through hill farming. Wordsworth idealized these human-made landscapes. For instance:

> A lover of the meadows and the woods,
> And mountains; and of all that we behold
> From this green earth; of all the mighty world
> Of eye, and ear, – both what they half create,
> And what perceive; well pleased to recognise
> In nature and the language of the sense
> The anchor of my purest thoughts, the nurse,
> The guide, the guardian of my heart, and soul
> Of all my moral being.
>
> (Wordsworth, 'Tintern Abbey', *Lyrical Ballads*, 1798)

For all of these writers and artists, the threat of creeping industrialism and its associated problems of pollution and environmental degradation were the most important consequences of industrial society. The first active pressure group to gain wider public support was formed in response to the proposal in the 1870s by the Manchester Corporation to build a dam across the Lake District valley of Thirlmere. This proposal was the product of the need for a more effective source of water to service the industrial needs of Manchester. The Thirlmere Defence Association conducted an effective campaign, defeating the Parliamentary bill in 1878 but failing to maintain this in the following year. The valley and the homes of its inhabitants were flooded to create a reservoir. The desires of the industrialists won but, in so doing, led to the creation of the Lake District Defence Society to counter the threat of further reservoirs and railway links. The campaign against railways highlights one of the contradictions of this movement. Rail transport provided access to beautiful natural settings for many who could not otherwise afford to live in the Lake District, whereas for the campaigners the presence of the working classes coming to visit the Lakes in large numbers would in itself spoil the landscape.

Whereas, in Britain, ecocentric and holistic thinking tended to confuse the natural with the human-made environment, in America, the experience of uncluttered and unaltered wilderness generated deeper stirrings in the human imagination. The frontier mentality of American society saw the wilderness as wasteland and the American Indians, the indigenous peoples living in harmony and balance with this environment, as savages who had failed to realize the benefits that more appropriate uses of land and natural resources could deliver. Even in the early settlements of the east coast of America, it had been widely believed that, in the absence of farming, the Indians had no legal property rights to the land they occupied. Ownership had been inextricably linked to treating natural things as having no other value than that attributed to how they served the needs and purposes of the settlers. This attitude towards nature can be seen as plausible and sensible in a society of free farmers and miners. The challenge posed by writers such as Henry David Thoreau and John Muir was a challenge to the fundamental values of their own society, as much as a defence of the increasingly encroached wilderness.

The naturalist writings of Thoreau provided a way of transforming the human appreciation of nature into a powerful political message which runs throughout ecological thought to the present day. Thoreau's accounts of his life in the wilderness and his travelogues provided descriptive catalogues of his encounters with the landscape and its occupants. He promoted the 'Arcadian' approach, which asserts the need for human beings to live in harmony with nature and opposes the 'imperialistic' view of natural things as existing purely for human benefit. He regarded the earth as a spiritual body and the source of life, a source which should not be violated by the search for monetary wealth. John Muir turned these insights into a more sharply focused set of demands for leaving a portion of the wilderness to one side of the exploitative and vandalizing tendencies of human beings. His writings chronicled the encroachments on the remaining wild areas in the late nineteenth century, which were increasing in terms of their frequency and impact. Of particular note was the escalating human demand for timber.

> In the noblest forests of the world, the ground, once divinely beautiful, is desolate and repulsive, like a face ravaged by disease. This is true also of many other Pacific coast and Rocky Mountain valleys and forests. The same fate, sooner or later, is awaiting them all, unless awakening public opinion comes forward to stop it.
>
> (Muir 1901: 5)

The continued existence of wilderness could only be secured through the creation of natural parks, by the deliberate action of the state. In this way, Muir argued, we could 'make the mountains glad'. On other matters, the sentiments of Thoreau were to have less of an impact. The increasing population density and the needs of agriculture in California led to massive pressure for the damming of the deep valleys of Yosemite. Muir found himself locked in a debate with the advocates of the management of natural resources for human use, rather than the preservation of ecosystems. The most significant advocate of the conservationist movement for human welfare was Gifford Pinchot (1901). Conservationism tends to moderate the pressures for an exploitative 'free for all' inherent in the drives which propel actions in economic markets. Nevertheless, the substitution of careful and prudent (that is, businesslike) management of natural resources, for the benefit of present and future human generations, changed the criteria for decisions affecting the forests and mountains in the American national parks. This was far removed from the preservationist approach of Thoreau and Muir.

The difference between these positions, between conservation and preservation, has helped to shape the debates and decisions about the green environment ever since. However, the relentless pressure for more living space, food, fuel and other raw materials which accompanies rapid population growth, has meant that the conservationist case has been the main means of restraining human infringements of the wild places. The limits of the conservationist case, which is a sort of fighting retreat against human encroachments, were already becoming apparent in the mid-twentieth century. Aldo Leopold's *A Sand County Almanac* (1949) identified these difficulties and argued that what was needed was not a curtailment of greed and material hypochondria in the name of the value of human welfare so much as a revaluation of values themselves. Rather than treating the land as a commodity, with the value of an acre plot identified in terms of a dollar price, Leopold asked us to consider the values of 'love, respect and admiration' for land, a land ethic. Part of the problem, he argued, stems from the way in which modern societies involve such a complex division of labour that many people do not come into contact with natural things except through carefully crafted scenery, tamed zoo animals and golf. Many simply do not encounter the free and untamed natural environment. For Leopold, the mechanization of society, including farming practices, has fundamentally transformed the ways in which land and the ecosystem are valued and understood.

Leopold's clarion call for a revaluation of values about nature came to fruition in the late 1960s and early 1970s, when the human impacts upon the green environment became more immediate and visible. Many of the landmark writings of this period of emerging ecological consciousness are mixed with a sense of possible ecological catastrophe. This was, in part, the product of the close connections between the environmental movements and the anti-nuclear and peace campaigns which focused heavily upon the possibility of human self-destruction. This was seen as an inherent feature of the military-industrial complex around which, it was argued, the goals of society were organized. The awakening of this ecological consciousness can be charted through a rapid succession of seminal works on human impacts on the environment, starting with Rachel Carson's *Silent Spring* (1962). Carson identifies the ways in which pesticides, in this case DDT, simply lead agricultural pests to develop their own resistance, as well as the ways in which the residues of pesticides concentrate in the food chain and consequently become dangerous for birds and animals higher up the food chain. The evocative title of the study stems from the disappearance of birds in areas where DDT use was intense. Certainly Carson's account raised two issues, that human activities can have dramatic and unanticipated consequences and that ecosystems were much more fragile than previously acknowledged.

Other landmarks in this period include *The Limits to Growth* (Meadows *et al.* 1972) and 'A Blueprint for Survival' (Goldsmith *et al.* 1972). The *Limits to Growth* report by the Club of Rome highlighted the ways in which human economic activities, in relation to resource depletion and pollution, were exceeding the carrying capacity of the earth and that the continuation of current practices was unsustainable in the long term. The 'Blueprint for Survival' report, written by the editorial collective of the *Ecologist* magazine, established the need for a reassessment of the ways in which cultural values and the social order would have to be altered if the ecological problems generated by complex industrial societies were to be resolved. The importance of these two studies stems from the way in which they recast the environmental agenda, by grounding the green critique in the problems of industrialism and the values of modern society. This enabled them to highlight the way in which the conventional politics of both left and right was founded upon materialism, economic growth for its own sake, and the instrumental view of natural things. The rapacious tendencies of capital accumulation and the massive pollution in the actually existing socialist societies of the Eastern bloc were manifestations of the same problem. In each case, it was now possible to identify a common culprit, industrialism. A sustainable society, it was argued, would have to be radically different and would involve a fundamental rethink about some of the basic questions, such as the role of the division of labour in the social order. In short, ecological thought is about transformation. While these studies of human impacts upon the environment have highlighted the risks and hazards involved in human activities, they also provide a context for the emergence of deep ecology.

Ecology and intrinsic value

Recent ecological thought has been profoundly influenced by Arne Naess, and, in particular, his account of the differences between shallow and 'deep ecology'. Naess argues that most forms of human knowledge are inherently anthropocentric and, as such, incapable of acknowledging the importance of the ecosystem except in so far as it serves human concerns. He also suggests that most green thought rests upon these assumptions. Naess argues that environmentalists who approach the issues of global warming and ozone depletion, with human values and interests as paramount, tend to treat natural things in an instrumental way and, as such, are 'shallow ecologists'. In its place he argues for a 'deep ecology' which recognizes that all life forms have an intrinsic value, that is, they have a value regardless of shifting human values. The measure of well-being should be the flourishing of all life rather than how something serves the purposes of human beings. In order to flourish life should be diverse, which is a value in itself. Naess suggests that the activities of human beings undermine this diversity and, if human beings were simply to satisfy their vital needs, social life would have to be altered dramatically. Most significantly, Naess argues that the carrying capacity of the earth demands a much smaller human population of around 100 million if, as a species, human beings are to have a sustainable future. For Naess, the belief in the intrinsic value of nature and the role of diversity in the flourishing of life create an obligation to act in order to change the existing state of affairs. One of the movements which adopts the 'deep ecology' viewpoint is Earth First, a direct action group which has used what have been described as ecoterrorist tactics. For example, by driving metal staves into American hard wood trees, they have made logging with chain-saws a very dangerous occupation. In practice, Naess has disowned such forms of political activity.

It is useful to explore the ideas of intrinsic value and diversity in more detail. John O'Neill provides us with a way of clarifying the arguments. The idea of identifying intrinsic value in all natural things is more problematic than Naess suggests. O'Neill argues that it can mean any combination of three different things. First, it can be taken broadly as opposed to instrumental valuation, that intrinsic value refers to the natural thing not as a means to an end but as an end in itself. It is this broad sense of intrinsic value which is used within this text. Second, intrinsic value can refer to the intrinsic properties or structure of the natural thing in question. Finally, intrinsic value can refer to the process of valuation itself, as an indication of objective value which exists in some way independently of the ways in which human beings value them. By posing the idea that valuation always takes place through social context and within a language system, the preceding sections on the way we see nature have already ruled out the identification of any intrinsic value of this kind. In any case, the idea of objectivity has shifted so many times and so frequently, that it is sensible to regard any such claims with suspicion. In identifying the operating principles of ecologism, it is only necessary to specify the first sense of intrinsic value as non-instrumental value, which is certainly the case in the work of Naess but not of all deep ecologists. Now, in relation to the principle of diversity, it is useful to examine the arguments of Naess directly. According to Naess:

> Diversity enhances the potentialities of survival, the chances of new modes of life, the richness of forms. And the so-called struggle for life, and survival of the fittest, should be interpreted in the sense of ability to co-exist and co-operate in complex relationships, rather than ability to kill, exploit and suppress. 'Live and let live' is one more powerful ecological principle than the 'Either you or me'.
>
> (Naess 1973: 96)

For Naess, shallow ecology reduces the 'multiplicity of life' (both within and beyond species) and deep ecology enhances it. O'Neill argues that this simplifies the issues involved and that biological diversity is good not in itself but for the 'stability and robustness of ecosystems' (O'Neill 1993: 99). He argues that we need to focus upon diversity within ecological communities, that is, diversity between species, a situation which is compatible with a lack of diversity within species. Finally, in contradiction to Naess's claim that deep ecology rests upon human cultural, economic and occupational diversity, O'Neill argues that the goal of a sustainable way of life automatically assumes that unsustainable ways of life (which tend to exceed the earth's carrying capacity) would have to disappear. This means that Western consumerist cultures and African cattle-based communities are in question.

It is possible that O'Neill is wilfully misreading Naess, for deep ecologists have always been clear about the broad constraints of sustainability within which human beings should operate. A sustainable social order, it is argued, would be much more small-scale and localized, a feature which would promote cultural diversity. In turn, sustainable local economies would have to be innovative in unexpected and unpredictable ways in order to find ways of substituting for goods which they could not ship across the globe. These tendencies, embodied in what Naess describes as the 'ecosophy' which constitutes the rules of conduct of everyday life, would promote diversity but only within definite ecological constraints. However, O'Neill is right to demand a clearer expression of basic principles from ecosophy or deep ecology. The appeals to intrinsic value and diversity do not sustain the critical and explanatory load piled upon them. Nevertheless, if cultural and economic diversity diminishes with the presence of a globalizing commercial capitalist economy (no matter how diverse human societies once were) and if such diversity is enhanced by sustainable localized human communities, then O'Neill should not simply reject the deep ecology position as a failed argument.

Already, certain broad themes about ecologism can be identified. Nature means many things to many different people, and this is reflected in the diverse positions highlighted throughout this book. All meaningful constructions of natural things are social creations and inevitably involve values. In general terms, it is possible to identify two broad positions on the way in which natural things are valued. On the one hand, it is possible to value natural things in terms of how they promote the good life for human beings, which assumes that human interests are paramount. Alternatively, it is possible to place human beings in a harmonious relationship with the ecosystem which sustains human life in the first place. This does not necessarily mean that human self-interest, in this case human survival, must be in danger to make such values relevant. However, given the propensity of human beings to ignore the warning signals of ecological change in the name of material self-interest, it seems inevitable that the idea of survival will become a major factor in the debates of the near future.

In Chapters 2 and 3 we will explore two recent debates about the ways in which natural things has been valued and the ways in which we should understand human impacts upon natural things. In Chapter 2 we will examine the arguments about our obligations to future generations, the most human-centred debate. In Chapter 3 we will explore the human treatment of non-human animals. These debates are useful in that they allow us to explore definite ethical approaches towards natural things and how much depends on the ways in which human beings define justice, entitlements and obligations. In Chapters 4 and 5, which explore the impact of ecological thought upon traditions in social and political theory, we will examine the ways in which these debates about justice, entitlements and obligations raise questions about the assumptions within liberalism, conservatism, socialism, anarchism and feminism when they encounter ecological thought. More generally, we will also examine what impact ecological thought has had in relation to the preferred social order of each tradition. In the concluding chapter, we will return to central themes in the text and assess the prospects for the emergence of ecological citizenship. More generally, this book aims to highlight the role of ethical thought in thinking about nature and what it means to us. This means that we should explore the shifting meanings of 'nature' and the 'natural' and how these have had an impact upon the debates about the environment. In this way it is possible to establish how the ways in which we discuss ethical issues underpin all accounts of natural things and how any attempt to alter the terms of reference of these discussions have to start with these in mind.

2 Obligations to Future Generations and Intergenerational Justice

The question of obligations is a difficult one. We prefer to talk about rights and entitlements, about what we can do for ourselves, rather than about obligations and duties, about what we should do for others. Obligations are often an afterthought, rather than the first thing we consider. Nevertheless, it is often the case that each bundle of rights carries with it a whole series of obligations. This brings us to the crucial question in relation to human impacts on environment: to whom and to what we are obliged. Conventional liberal ethics has a particular focus upon the way we define the boundary of the moral community. Membership of the moral community carries with it both entitlements and obligations. For instance, membership of contemporary societies means that each individual has certain rights regarding free speech and assembly as well as welfare rights. Nevertheless, there are a series of corresponding obligations regarding the limits on free speech (such as laws on libel and slander), the need for public order and the expectation that employed individuals will pay taxation to finance welfare provision. The welfare example raises a relevant way of thinking through some of the problems addressed in this chapter. Welfare involves the recognition of the needs of strangers in a way that private philanthropy does not, for it expresses our obligations to all other members of our society.

On the needs of future strangers

Entitlements and obligations are considered to be relevant only to those who can be considered to be members of this moral community. The membership criterion has often been defined in terms of species membership, in this case the human species. In practice, it is quite difficult to identify an unquestionable foundation for this boundary. For instance, many animals possess the attributes of many humans. The difficulties this poses will be explored more in the next chapter. The present chapter will focus upon the obligations that present generations have towards future generations. In this case we should focus upon how we define the boundary within the human species. The status of children and those individuals who are considered, in one way or another, as 'mentally unfit', presents difficulties for conventional ethics if membership depends upon full use of 'rational faculties'. In a similar way, future generations, whether these are our immediate successors or distant future generations, raise interesting questions in relation to our present obligations. Future generations are potential people, for our actions in the present will determine which potential people can come into existence. We can begin to formulate questions with these issues in mind. Can we regard future generations as members, like children, so that in the meantime we should act as their guardians? In what ways can we balance our present needs with the needs of future strangers? How much of the earth's finite resources can we set aside or how much pollution can we avoid in the name of establishing an acceptable level of intergenerational justice? If we accept that the waste we are presently producing will be around and dangerous for a long time, then we have to consider the effect on potential people. Nuclear waste is likely to be a danger for a million years, therefore in this case we should consider the implications for about 30,000 generations.

A comparison is often made between the relationship between present and future generations and how we see the relationship between Western moral communities and the needs of strangers in other parts of the globe. The argument for Western overseas aid is, in part, based upon self-interest – that overseas aid is necessary to avoid instability, maintain supplies of important resources and even for the maintenance of markets for Western-manufactured products. Nevertheless, overseas aid is also justified in more general terms of the obligation, placed upon all members of humanity, to address the needs of strangers who are unable to meet their own needs. Famine relief is often addressed solely in these terms. Similarly, future generations can be seen to be equally worthy of such obligations on the grounds that, as part of humanity, their needs should be taken into consideration. Indeed, it could be argued that these obligations should be taken more seriously because the condition of future generations is a direct product of the decisions and activities of present generations. Present generations will be largely responsible for the benefits and harms experienced by future generations.

The example of the long-lasting impacts of nuclear waste has already indicated some of the difficulties which future generations will have to face. Resource depletion and pollution will have a wide range of effects upon future conditions. Specifically, a slow build-up of levels of chemical toxicity from industrial activities in the mid- to late twentieth century has begun to manifest itself. The side-effects of the presence of 'oestrogen-like compounds' in the water supply (derived from products such as household paint) are already altering the sexual balance of many species. In addition, this has been tentatively linked with declining human sperm counts and the rise of congenital abnormalities in male human offspring in western Europe. In a similar way, the difficulties raised by genetic engineering of plants and animals are likely to have a substantial effect upon the extent of biodiversity. In instrumental terms alone, the existence of diversity is essential to future human uses of natural things and yet agricultural practices are undermining this. A series of plantation crop disasters due to infestation were aggravated because of the uniformity of the crops involved. Immunity from the infestations was achieved through cross-breeding the genetically modified plants with wild varieties of the same plants. Once the conditions for biodiversity are eliminated, this option will no longer exist. Rather than present generations passing on a rich and diverse range of potential crops, future generations are likely to inherit a narrow selection of genetically modified plant types.

The recognition of obligations to future generations differs in certain fundamental ways from the ways in which we recognize our relations with our contemporaries. Whereas contemporary moral communities are based upon an equality of status, the relationship between present and future generations involves an unequal relationship in two senses. The first is inequality of power, for generally the activities of present generations can only do things to benefit or harm future generations, while the latter can only affect us in so far as they assess our reputations in posterity. Future generations cannot directly harm or benefit present generations in a material sense. The second sense is inequality of knowledge, for present generations have little awareness of the impact of their activities on the lives of future generations. This means that existing generations tend to weigh the positive and negative consequences of present activities more heavily than the consequences in the future. For instance, in environmental economics, it is common to engage in the practice of attributing a monetary value to environmental impacts such as the extraction of raw materials or the costs of repairing ecological damage. In particular, the comparison of costs and benefits is built into the assumptions of environmental economics. In relation to estimating the costs and benefits of large-scale projects which operate for a considerable time, it is also common to discount the costs and benefits of the project in future years. This operates in a similar way to the practice of discounting in insurance. It is assumed that our ignorance of the future and the risks involved in identifying costs and benefits in future years means that they should be weighed less heavily the further we estimate them into the future.

When we look at how we examine the costs and benefits of large-scale energy projects we can see some of the implications of this practice. All energy projects have large start-up costs, although some have greater short-run costs in terms of immediate ecological change and damage. While nuclear power stations tend to have massive short-term costs, these are adequately compensated for by the benefits of cheap nuclear power in the medium term, during the operational life of the power stations. However, there are very large costs in the long term because of the difficulties involved in the decommissioning of nuclear power stations and the storage of nuclear waste. By comparison, tidal barrages and windmill plantations involve considerable immediate impact upon the ecosystems in which they are located and which are only likely to be offset in the medium term. The benefits of these projects, particularly cheap renewable power, are much more apparent in the long term because there is little waste and the costs are limited to routine maintenance and updating of machinery. In the case of nuclear power, discounting decreases the weighting of the large long-term costs, whereas in the case of alternative renewable energy projects, discounting decreases their long-term benefits. The proliferation of nuclear power stations in the mid- to late twentieth century and the scarcity of renewable energy projects is a testament to the consequences of discounting. This raises important questions about whether present generations are acting in a just way towards future generations.

Intergenerational justice

The idea of justice provides social life with its underlying normative order, for it acts as the point of reference for defining appropriate behaviour within that community. The concept of justice rests upon the idea of regard for and fairness towards other members of the same moral community. Justice is an essentially contested concept and, as such, is ineradicably evaluative (Lukes 1974). The concept of justice serves as an important reference point for establishing the core values of a moral community or, for that matter, a particular social theory. There is a clear difference between the arguments in favour of social justice and advocating individual justice. So, rather than seeing justice as something fixed, we can examine the various ways in which it is defined in order to highlight the limits and possibilities of each approach. When we examine justice we are, in effect, examining the horizon of our moral considerations. This can be illustrated by focusing upon the way in which John Rawls develops the argument for a 'just savings principle'. This serves as a means of resolving some of the difficulties in dealing with the impact of human activities on the environment and of understanding the legacy we leave for our descendants.

The concept of justice provides a way of working out the principles upon which a social contract between all members of a moral community can be established. In *A Theory of Justice* (1971), Rawls focuses our attention on the question of the sort of society in which we would like to live. He constructs a scenario in which all members of a moral community are placed in a situation before any social arrangements have been fixed. This position he describes as the 'original position', behind the 'veil of ignorance'. Initially we will assume that the moral community is composed of present generations. In this original position, Rawls asks us to consider 'what sort of society would we consider to be just?', before we have any idea about what position or attributes we would hold in this society. In this hypothetical mind game, we are put in a position where we have to describe in advance how egalitarian our own society should be even though we have no idea whether we would be placed at the top or the bottom of the society we choose to construct. In such a situation, rational actors would opt for a social contract which is broadly egalitarian just in case they are placed at the bottom of that society. However, this could pose some difficulties if we created a society in which we all received the same rewards despite the variation in the form and intensity of the effort we put in. In a strictly equal society, there are few incentives for self-improvement. In order to address this without contradicting the first decision, he introduces the 'difference principle'. This permits individual members of the moral community to pursue self-interested actions, but only in so far as these actions also benefit the least well-off. A 'just social contract', according to Rawls, would be one in which the benefits of material progress were spread throughout society and in which the lowest in the social hierarchy were not left out. Rawls is, in effect, identifying a redistributive social order as a just one, rather than the inegalitarian social orders which tend to characterize Western industrial societies.

In considering whether our actions are just in relation to future generations, it only remains to extend the moral community from actually existing generations to include future generations as well. In this way we should consider what sort of relationship present generations should have with future generations, if we did not know which generation we would be in. The argument developed by Rawls stops short of this, for he only goes so far as recognizing the ties of sentiment between present and future generations. Rawls devises the 'just savings principle' to address the ways in which present actions could harm the interests of future generations. The idea of 'just savings' refers to the setting aside of natural assets in the same way as responsible decisions by a generation of a family should ensure the security of the next generation. This means that each generation should not start off in a situation worse than the previous generation. In this way, present generations should leave a share of finite natural resources and an environment which is largely unspoilt for future generations to enjoy. However, it is difficult to decide exactly what share of finite resources can be exploited for present needs and what should be left for future generations. Much depends upon how many generations we should wish to consider in this calculation. The more future generations we include, the more the share of finite natural resources which we can presently exploit shrinks. In this account of justice, we should refrain from actions which are likely to have adverse effects on others.

The view of justice developed by Rawls has been most notably challenged by the anarchist individualism of Robert Nozick. In *Anarchy, State and Utopia* (1974), Nozick argues that a just outcome is one which follows from a series of individual voluntary contracts regardless of whether the outcome is broadly equal or not. This approach assumes that the entitlements enjoyed by individuals are inviolable. Nozick draws upon the natural rights of life, limb and property identified by John Locke. The acquisition and possession of private property is identified as an important component of a free individualistic social order. To demonstrate the extent of each individual's obligations to others, Nozick uses the analogy that every individual is an island. The impact which each individual has upon others is conveyed through the metaphor of sea currents between islands. The activities in each case may create a range of impacts and the side-effects may be carried from one place to another. A key characteristic of the condition of anarchy is the assumption that each individual is free from authority. However, it is possible to establish authority, if it is based entirely on the consent of all those involved, and for all members to be able to renounce it, if their consent is no longer forthcoming. In addition, it should not infringe natural liberties such as private property. Consequently, the impact of environmental pollution places no obligation on polluters to clean up the effects of their activities, unless it infringes such natural liberties. In such situations, where damage to private property has occurred from pollution, the owner of the affected property is entitled to seek some form of compensation. In this account, present generations have no obligations towards future generations. For Nozick, no principle of justice can be legitimately established which would require that a proportion of existing resources should be set aside for our successors to use. Since potential people are not yet alive and cannot be said to be owners of property, they possess no entitlement which we can respect and claims for compensation are not valid.

So far we have contrasted two approaches towards intergenerational justice with very different assumptions about what constitutes a social contract. In the case of Rawls, we are justified in recognizing obligations to future generations, especially if we include future generations in the 'original position'. Rawls applies the contractarian assumptions of Kant, that if something is to be applied at all, it must apply to all members of the moral community. However, in Nozick's account, obligations to future generations are not binding because future human generations fall beyond the restricted criteria for membership of the moral community. It remains possible to justify obligatory commitments to a limited number of generations on a variety of grounds. If we retain the individual as the focus of analysis and regard obligations as limited to our own immediate descendants, it can be argued that each successive generation represents a 50 per cent reduction in our own genetic legacy and a corresponding reduction in obligations. Similarly, arguments for limited obligations based on the protection of family inheritance are usually left to a single blood line rather than all future offspring. The principle of primogeniture establishes that the eldest male has certain entitlements with regard to the inheritance of the assets of a family and, with that, a corresponding series of obligations to manage those assets for the benefit of future generations.

Selective obligations

Martin P. Golding developed a case for selective obligations to future generations, based on the cultural values of present generations. Golding argues that if we disapprove of the values of future generations, then no obligations exist. Golding's argument is interesting for it explicitly considers the nature of obligations as well as the boundaries within which they apply. He clearly addresses the difference between obligations to our contemporaries and to those who cannot share a 'common life'. Nevertheless, he finds the exclusion of all future generations unjustifiable because it fails to differentiate between the various forms which communities of the future can take. If some future generations were identical to present generations in terms of the values they hold then some obligation to them must exist. If this is the case, Golding argues, then such obligations are, by definition, connected to the 'rights' of future generations. Such future generations still have claims upon present generations even though they cannot literally make claims upon the living. Whether such claims are tantamount to rights, he argues, depends upon whether they originate from other members of the same moral community.

Golding accepts that the boundary of a moral community is always under threat from new claims for recognition and attempts at exclusion. Such disagreements are an expression of values as to who is worthy of consideration and who is not. This is the nub of the questions over obligations to future generations. For Golding, obligations to strangers are unclear in any case and a good guideline is to examine whether there is sufficient 'fellow-feeling' to warrant an obligation. This 'fellow-feeling' extends beyond 'sympathy' and 'mindless altruism' for it involves the expression of 'genuine concern and interest' in the condition of others so that there is an awareness of what would be good for them. This implies that if we are not in a position to empathize with other people and understand their conditions of life, then our minimal obligation would be to avoid interference. In any case, they may hold very different conceptions of the good life from our own. Golding does not see this relationship as a 'catalogue of rights' but as a responsible attitude, in the same way as the responsibility for promoting the 'good' of the child which exists for parents. Specific obligations then follow as an expression of this basic principle.

When we apply these principles to the relationship between present and future generations, Golding suggests that we do have an obligation to our immediate successors, to our born and unborn children. In these cases we may wish to conserve the natural landscape, so that it provides as much pleasure for them as it does for present generations. However, when confronted with the issue of further obligations to future strangers, Golding argues:

> The more distant the generation we focus upon, the less likely it is that we have an obligation to promote its good. We would be both ethically and practically well-advised to set our sights on more immediate generations and, perhaps, solely upon our immediate posterity. After all, even if we do have obligations to future generations, our obligations are undoubtedly much clearer. The nearer the generations are to us, the more likely it is that our conception of the good life is relevant to them. There is certainly enough work for us to do in discharging our responsibility to promote a good life for them. But it would be

> unwise, both from an ethical and a practical perspective, to seek to promote the good of the very distant.
>
> (Golding 1972: 98)

Reconsidering the earlier example in this chapter on meeting the needs of strangers through overseas and humanitarian aid, Western governments usually apply some criteria of selection. It has been common to select societies as deserving on the basis of the affinity which they have with Western values. For example, American humanitarian aid has been denied on the basis of poor human rights records and the ideological beliefs of a number of governments. Such arguments would limit obligations by being selective about the kind of future generations to which present generations would be obligated and, in Golding's case, there is a cut-off point at which obligations should end. Other arguments which develop such selective criteria for moral consideration, however, focus more on the number of generations to which we have obligations and hold that present generations are only obliged to all members of those so selected.

In *Man's Responsibility for Nature* (1974), John Passmore develops a case for consideration of and obligations to our immediate posterity, based upon what we love. This is in part derived from Golding but also draws upon the insights of the utilitarian approach, developed by Jeremy Bentham and John Stuart Mill, for drawing our attention to the consequences of human actions. The utilitarian approach focuses upon the promotion of collective human happiness or welfare and seeks to identify the ways in which pain can be minimized and pleasure can be maximized. Some of the decisions we make have contradictory consequences, that is, they can involve negative consequences for some and positive consequences for others; they may even have both positive and negative consequences for each individual. In such a situation, utilitarians argue, we need to compare the various consequences of our actions and come to a decision as to whether the consequences provide grounds for acting or not acting. This means that we have to find ways of measuring such consequences in order to make decisions which maximize human happiness. When this is applied to the future, considerable problems can be identified in measuring the likely future consequences of present actions. Because of the uncertainties involved in predicting the future, utilitarians tend to weigh unknown consequences less heavily than known outcomes, as in the illustration of discounting techniques earlier in this chapter. Passmore recognizes the uncertainties involved in calculating likely consequences, when he argues that we do not know for certain that 'a beggar will not choke on the bread we offer' (Passmore 1974: 50). He draws the conclusion that obligations should be limited to immediate posterity.

The utilitarian case for the limitation of obligations to our immediate descendants fits Passmore's own argument that we can only love a limited number of generations of our own offspring. He argues that we cannot love what we do not know and understand. This means that future uncertainties are a key criterion for identifying obligations. Consequently, since we cannot love beyond our immediate posterity we have no obligations towards distant future generations. However, if we were to apply this criteria to present conditions, which are complex and uncertain as well, then claims to obligations within existing moral communities are also undermined. Brian Barry argues against this position:

> Of course, we don't know what the precise tastes of our remote descendants will be, but they are unlikely to include a desire for skin cancer, soil erosion, or the inundation of low-lying areas as a result of the melting of the ice-caps.
>
> (Barry 1977: 274)

Such arguments seem to rest upon a common position regarding what we can know and understand about the present condition and the ethical standards appropriate towards it. They imply that the present is simple rather than complex, certain rather than uncertain, and static rather than changing. In fact both the present and the future are characterized by complexity, uncertainty and change. Barry's argument applies as much to the here and now as to the distant future.

Rethinking intergenerational obligations

The case developed by Richard and Val Routley draws upon the recognition that we should treat the conditions of future generations in the same way as we would consider the conditions of the living. In this 'intuitionist' approach, the attempt to draw any boundary between present generations, immediate posterity and even distant future generations is fundamentally mistaken. To demonstrate this, they developed the powerful analogy of the intergenerational bus journey. They ask us to consider a bus on a very long journey carrying both passengers and goods. The bus stops at various points on its long journey and the passengers and driver change a great number of times. At some point someone places a package on the bus for a destination towards the end of the journey. This package contains

> a highly toxic and explosive gas . . . packaged in a very thin container, which as the consignor well knows is unlikely to contain the gas for the full distance for which it is consigned, and certainly will not do so if the bus should encounter any trouble, for example if there is a breakdown and the interior of the bus becomes very hot, if the bus should strike a very large bump . . . or if some passenger should interfere deliberately or inadvertently with the cargo or perhaps try to steal some of the freight, as also frequently happens. All of these things, let us suppose, have happened on some of the bus's previous journeys. If the container should break, the resulting disaster would probably kill at least some of the people and animals on the bus, while others could be maimed or contract serious diseases.
>
> (Routley and Routley 1978: 133)

This analogy of a bus journey for intergenerational storage of chemical and nuclear waste is geared to prompt an intuitive response from the reader. The act of placing this package appears to be without regard for its potential impact on others, particularly in the future. What Routley and Routley wish to emphasize with this analogy is the standard way in which the long-term storage of toxic and radioactive waste is defended in contemporary Western societies. Such defences range from the complacent belief that the unexpected troubles and consequent leaks are unlikely, to the view that those on the bus might have an accident anyway or die before the package becomes dangerous. They may even go as far as to suggest that it is the responsibility of the passengers and the driver to ensure that the journey is a smooth one. Alternately, it is possible to dehumanize the victims of the leak, by suggesting that their harm is of little or no consequence. These arguments would appear to be unacceptable, yet they have been used in one way or another in defending the storage of toxic chemicals and nuclear waste. It should not be a surprise to discover that waste is often stored in environments which contained marginalized social groups or in developing societies.

Routley and Routley identify the most common justification as a business imperative. The productive process inevitably results in such wastes, which have to be stored somewhere. This is usually couched in terms of 'all industry produces waste' and, since we do not wish to be a pre-industrial society, we are stuck with the problem. The assumption that waste is inevitable is often combined with the argument that all opponents of, say, nuclear waste dumps, are simply engaged in 'nimby' politics (that is, 'not in my backyard'). In particular, Routley and Routley argue that the risks involved in the long-term dumping of nuclear waste closely match this bus journey analogy in terms of the moral dilemmas and the excuses used to justify dumping of the nuclear waste and associated contaminated materials. The time-span for the storage of the massive amount of waste produced is estimated to be in excess of a thousand years, and for plutonium much longer. The safe storage of this waste requires constant human maintenance and has to take into account the possibility of long-term changes in climate, geology and possible disturbance. The transformation of human lives over the last few thousand years gives a good indication of the uncertainties involved. All this waste, they argue, is equivalent to a thousand Hiroshimas produced from each power station each year, for just thirty years of power. In addition, the potential catastrophic consequences from a relatively small leak are huge. According to Routley and Routley, the legacy for future generations is twofold. Nuclear waste is still going to present a burden in terms of its careful storage. We have also, as a consequence of present energy orientations, initiated a form of global development based on high resource use and high energy use. This will make any attempt to convert the future global economy towards renewable energy sources even more difficult than today. Routley and Routley conclude with the recognition that 'time bombs with long fuses', such as nuclear waste and toxic chemicals, are morally unacceptable solely in terms of their effects on the future.

We can see from these positions, that there are intense disputes over the extent and nature of our obligations to future generations. When present generations make decisions and engage in activities with beneficial short-term consequences, but which could seriously harm or burden people in the long term, they are discriminating against future generations. The existence of a moral boundary between present and future generations of human beings is hard to substantiate. This is a reflection of the way in which the idea of a moral community is open to contestation. In addition, there are disagreements as to whether we should discuss these issues in terms of 'a just system of rules' or in terms of 'human happiness', as well as disputes as to what these mean. I wish to argue that, in practice, all the criteria used to identify the conditions of future generations, in order to justify the privilege of the already existent, are also characteristic of present generations. If the same moral dilemmas apply to potential people and our contemporaries, then the case developed by Routley and Routley is strengthened. Certainly, this means that we should not discriminate against future generations, although it does not help us to work out what the impacts will be, so far in the future.

This means that we at least need an initial set of new guidelines which will serve to avoid some of the problems identified above and make sensible decisions between alternative courses of inaction and action. Daniel Callahan (1971) provides four useful guidelines on avoiding future jeopardy, which express greater respect for future generations and which have been adapted slightly for the purposes of this chapter:

1 Present generations should not act in ways which jeopardize the existence of future generations.
2 Present generations should not act in ways which jeopardize the ability of future generations to live in dignity.
3 Present generations, in defence of their own interests, may have to act in ways which jeopardize future generations but should do so in ways which minimize this risk.
4 In attempting to determine whether present activities do jeopardize the existence or dignity of future generations, present generations should act in responsible and sensitive ways as if each action with uncertain consequences could harm one's own children.

In each guideline, it is assumed that human beings who are alive should act with restraint in case they harm human beings who are not yet alive. These guidelines provide a basis for fostering a new attitude towards potential people. However, this remains an anthropocentric criterion, which limits moral consideration to human beings and ignores claims for consideration by non-human animals and other natural things. Many of the same problems and issues developed in relation to future generations are relevant in the debates on animal welfare and animal rights. It is to the problems and issues raised by placing animals within the moral community that we now turn.

3
Human and Non-human Animals

This chapter explores one of the most emotive and controversial issues in environmental ethics. The conditions in which animals live and the treatment of animals by human beings have recently provoked intense discussion. The issues of hunting, vivisection and vegetarianism have become the most passionate areas of conviction politics. A whole range of human practices and institutions have been called into question. This has produced a lively debate about the ethical system that underpins societies which engage in the use of animals for human needs and purposes, with little or no consideration of the implications of this for animals themselves. When we raise questions about whether or not human beings should eat meat, wear furs, laugh at monkeys confined in a cage or elephants standing on their hind legs in a circus, we are also raising questions about the very way of life in those societies. In short, this chapter addresses the debates about whether we should consider non-human animals in moral discussion and, if so, on what grounds human beings should attribute moral consideration to them. In particular, this chapter focuses upon whether animal suffering is the key issue or whether animals have an intrinsic value which endows them with rights and entitlements to which human beings have obligations.

The recent wave of activism in the UK on this issue can be dated from the early 1960s alongside other environmental movements which emerged at this time. The publication of Ruth Harrison's *Animal Machines* (1964) and its serialization in *The Observer* newspaper raised public awareness about animal welfare and the effects of factory farming. Of particular concern were the ways in which animals were confined within small pens with little room for physical movement and deprived of light. Such intensive farming practices came under scrutiny in the Brambell Committee on Animal Welfare. The Brambell Report (1965) recommended that both the physical and mental well-being of farm animals had to be taken into account in farming. The Report stated that each animal should be able to turn round, groom itself, get up, lie down and stretch its limbs as well as specifically recommending better lighting, a ban on the bleeding of veal calves and the end of mutilations, such as the debeaking of chickens and the docking of pigs' tails. While the specific recommendations were implemented, the general recommendations on confinement were ignored. The establishment of the Farm Animal Welfare Advisory Committee, in 1967, with the power to identify codes of practice which were designed to improve the conditions of animals, appeared to allay concerns but then simply enshrined existing practices within the codes. The weakness of legislative regulation and the backtracking from the Brambell Report caused considerable frustration among animal activists. By the late 1970s, more direct protest movements began to emerge. At the same time, the plight of animals began to receive more serious consideration in ethical debates.

Utilitarianism and animal suffering

The debates between philosophers on the role of human beings in relation to non-human animals became the ideological debating ground for the diverse parts of these direct action movements. Peter Singer's seminal book on *Animal Liberation* (1976) marks an important watershed in the level and complexity of discussion. Singer placed the issue of the treatment of animals squarely on the agenda by challenging the prevailing consensus that if farming practices were causing suffering then the animals would not thrive in the first place. This view had been promoted very successfully in government departments and the media through the activities of the livestock farming lobby. One effect of the Brambell Report had been the introduction in 1968 of a legal definition of animal suffering as 'unnecessary pain or unnecessary distress'. Singer drew upon the utilitarian tradition in philosophy in order to demonstrate the ways in which the idea of suffering deserved much more close scrutiny than it had previously received. In addition, it remained to be demonstrated where the boundary between necessary and unnecessary pain and distress actually lay, if it could be demonstrated at all.

Later, in *Practical Ethics* (1993) Singer starts from the assumption that the principle of equality is the 'principle of equal consideration of interests' and that this has served as the basis of moral debates on the status of all human beings. In particular, he stresses that all people should have the opportunity to live their lives to the full. He uses the experiences of marginalized groups, excluded from the benefits of a full life on the grounds of gender, ethnicity and disability, to demonstrate how the equal consideration of interests can overcome the prejudices of sexism, racism and ableism. In each case the denial of an opportunity on the grounds of physical characteristics is a discriminatory act. Each is grounded in a particular form of prejudice. For Singer, the belief that human animals are somehow superior to non-human animals as a justification for any treatment of animals, no matter how much suffering is inflicted, is just such a prejudice. Just as in racism, where the interests of black people are not taken seriously, so in speciesism the interests of animals are not taken seriously or are even ignored. Singer argues that human beings are often guilty of this sort of prejudice, in the same way as the support of slavery often went unquestioned as a fact of life in the eighteenth and nineteenth centuries.

> The argument for extending the principle of equality beyond our species . . . implies that our concern for others ought not to depend on what they are like, or what abilities they possess. . . . It is on this basis that we are able to say that the fact that some people are not members of our race does not entitle us to exploit them, and similarly the fact that some people are less intelligent than others does not mean that their interests can be disregarded.
>
> (Singer 1993: 56)

Drawing from the utilitarian philosopher, Jeremy Bentham, Singer argues that it is not a matter of whether animals can engage in rational thought or whether they can communicate through language, it is simply a matter of whether they can suffer. From this perspective, any account of the equal consideration of interests must start from the questions raised by examining the capacity for suffering and enjoyment; only by dealing with these characteristics can interests have any meaning at all.

Singer then goes on to acknowledge the ways in which the capacity for suffering varies from being to being. This draws upon the qualitative form of utilitarianism developed by John Stuart Mill, whereby a person with intelligence and sensitivity has a greater capacity for both enjoyment and suffering than someone lacking these qualities. This argument had played a central part in Mill's case for meritocracy, with the more intelligent individuals receiving a voting entitlement in proportion to their level of education. For Singer, it is only possible to compare realistically the pain felt by a mouse and the pain experienced by a human being by recognizing these different capacities for suffering. In addition, he suggests, animals cannot anticipate their fate, whereas a terminally ill human being is conscious of approaching death and can have a greater knowledge of what the process of dying involves. This means that human beings suffer in ways that animals do not. Singer is concerned with the total or aggregate consequences of a particular situation. He calculates that, if we are faced with the situation where we have to choose between experimenting with a new treatment upon a person and placing a mouse within a medical experiment, then it would be more appropriate to experiment on a mouse than on a human being. Beyond such simplistic choices, Singer stresses that the consequences of each situation have to be measured carefully in order to ascertain the best possible outcome for all those affected. Thus, for Singer, it is quite feasible that the benefits to a small number of human beings from, say, medical experimentation may outweigh the suffering of a large number of animals, so that the aggregate outcome is positive. According to utilitarian calculations, the infliction of suffering upon animals may be considered to be legitimate in some circumstances.

It is in relation to these different qualities displayed by different beings that the most powerful aspect of Singer's argument is developed. Once we accept this criterion as the sole means for making such judgements, in terms of this framework disturbingly it is also possible to consider human infants and intellectually disabled adult human beings as eligible for human experimentation on exactly the same grounds. The condemnation of National Socialist experimentation on Jewish children and the 'mentally unfit' clearly demonstrates the repugnance felt about such actions within conventional ethics. This contradiction leads into Singer's central argument against speciesism. If we exclude non-human animals from moral consideration on the grounds that they do not possess the capacity for rational thought and language skills, we also remove part of our own species from moral consideration. This would logically contradict the argument that all human animals are superior to non-human animals. Singer accepts that precise calculations of suffering will be impossible to identify with accuracy, but suggests that even if human beings were not to be affected in any way comparable to the effects on animals, the transformation would be enormous in any case.

> We would be forced to make radical changes in our treatment of animals that would involve our diet, the farming methods we use, the experimental procedures in many fields of sciences, our approach to wildlife and to hunting, trapping and the wearing of furs, and areas of entertainment like circuses, rodeos, and zoos. As a result, the total quantity of suffering caused would be greatly reduced; so greatly that it is hard to imagine any other change of moral attitude that would cause so great a reduction in the total sum of suffering in the universe.
> (Singer 1993: 61)

Singer contends that eating meat for survival, as in the diets of Arctic peoples, differs fundamentally from the consumption of meat by people generally, for we can still experience healthy lives on a vegetarian diet. In addition, the end of meat eating would lead to a more efficient use of agricultural resources and produce more food, because of the end of the wasteful process of feeding grain to livestock. In particular, vegetarianism ends the misery that animals experience in intensive farming. The second area of concern for Singer is the use of animals in research experimentation. In particular, he focuses upon the standardization procedures in the tests on animals for measuring toxicity levels in food additives. These tests routinely result in the death of half of the samples of animals used. In addition, he highlights the Draize test, which involves the deposit of chemicals in droplets into the eyes of animals in order to identify the likelihood of skin irritation for human beings.

The killing of animals presents a range of difficulties for utilitarians, for this approach could view the end of life as a reduction in suffering. Singer raises evidence of rudimentary speech in primates which can demonstrate that apes have expectations and purposes. In any case, the forms of communication between animals as well as their capacities for problem-solving exceed the capacities of young human beings. In this way, if we accept that to be a person there must be the capacity for rational and self-conscious thought, intentional actions and communication, then some non-human animals are also persons. Consequently, if it is wrong to kill persons then this also applies to non-human persons such as apes, dogs, cats, cattle and so on. However, as far as animals which do not possess the characteristics of persons are concerned, utilitarian considerations apply. This will reflect the way in which animals are killed, the extent of suffering involved and whether the killing is 'humane'. Singer concludes that the killing of fish (where the fish stocks are replaced) may not be considered morally wrong in certain circumstances. The utilitarian argument would also allow for some meat eating, but certainly not factory farming, where the animals have experienced suffering. Singer concludes that there are considerable practical problems involved in ensuring that animals have not suffered, especially if animal welfare is to be sustained to agreed standards. He argues that it would be easier in practice to avoid meat eating altogether, unless it were a matter of survival. He regards vegetarianism as a sort of litmus test of human respect for animals. If human beings gave up eating animals, it would herald the emergence of a new attitude whereby animals are no longer seen as simply there for human beings to use. The response to Singer's argument was prompt and fierce. In the following sections we will address these responses, starting with Tom Regan's *The Case for Animal Rights* (1984).

On obligations to animals

Tom Regan developed a case for animal rights by drawing upon the Kantian conception of justice. For Regan, once we recognize that all animals have certain fundamental moral rights, then human beings are forced to transform their attitudes towards the treatment of non-human animals. In certain respects the moral position of non-human animals is unique, for they do not possess the means to defend these rights. Regan launches his argument from an examination of the way in which a human being consumes thousands of animals in a lifetime. In order to sustain the practice of meat eating, in a complex and highly populated society, a very large meat-producing industry has to exist. He suggests that this has to be addressed in the utilitarian calculations involved in assessing the prospects for vegetarianism. The interests of millions of persons involved in the meat industry, in terms of capital investment or employment, also have to be included in the calculation of pleasure and enjoyment that Singer constructs.

For Regan, Singer's work contains a deep paradox in relation to this issue. This paradox logically follows from the core assumptions of utilitarianism. Singer's strategy rests upon the hope that human beings will eventually come to recognize that the way in which animals are treated creates unnecessary suffering and, in addition, is an inefficient way of producing food. However, as Regan suggests, the meat industry will not evaporate through this process, for all meat eaters would have to do is to 'eat more meat'. In this way, the collective impact of the growth of vegetarianism would be negated by the increase in the intensity of meat consumption, leaving the existing factors in the utilitarian calculus unaltered. Regan sketches out an alternative approach which changes the way in which non-human animals are understood. To do this, Regan extends the idea of a moral community to include animals and, in so doing, attributes the idea of intrinsic value to non-human as well as human animals. This means that 'all animals are equal', as Singer suggested, but not in terms of the 'equal consideration of interests'. For Regan, all animals are ends in themselves rather than the means to some set of human ends. As members of the moral community, non-human animals have rights in the same way as human beings have rights.

Regan and Singer pose the possibility of an extensive transformation of the human treatment of non-human animals. In response, a whole series of writers and philosophers have attempted to support the status quo. Most have focused upon the differences between human and non-human animals as grounds for not considering the suffering or the rights of animals. One of the most significant advocates of this view, Raymond Frey, argues that sentiency alone does not provide an indisputable basis for attributing rights. By this argument only human beings have the capacity for autonomous moral choices and, thus, only humans have interests. Frey argues that desires depend upon having beliefs and these, in turn, depend upon having a language system. Since animals do not have language and beliefs, he argues, they do not possess the capacity for desires. Consequently, he concludes that animals have needs but not desires, unlike human beings (see Frey 1980). For Regan, this argument involves a series of false steps, for children clearly believe something to be true before and during the acquisition of language skills. It is also plausible to think of children having desires for objects prior to any beliefs about the objects or the world in which the objects exist. Regan summarizes the mental life of animals very effectively:

> Perception, memory, desire, belief, self-consciousness, intention, a sense of the future – these are among the leading attributes of the mental life of normal mammalian animals aged one or more. Add to this list the not unimportant categories of emotion (e.g. fear and hatred) and sentience, understood as the capacity to experience pleasure and pain, and we begin to approach a fair rendering of the mental life of these animals.
>
> (Regan 1984: 81)

Regan distinguishes his own rights approach from the prevalent views on the relationship between human and non-human animals which emphasize human duties. When considering the arguments about human obligations to non-human animals, he makes a useful distinction between indirect and direct duty views of the moral status of animals. Direct duty views, such as that developed by Singer, focus upon the moral rightness or wrongness of human decisions and actions in terms of their immediate consequences for non-human animals. In Singer's case, human beings have a duty not to inflict pain and suffering upon other animals. Indirect duty views, however, involve the recognition of obligations to animals on the grounds that we have a duty to the human species to behave in a certain way (such as environmental efforts to save rare species) or possibly a duty to some divine being, but not to the animals themselves. He identifies both Kant and Rawls as examples of the view that the good treatment of animals is likely to rub off on the ways in which human beings treat each other. Rawls excludes consideration of non-human animals from the 'original position' and thus excludes them from the consideration one receives by being a member of the same moral community. However, if we were to decide on the principles of the moral order without knowing what animal we were going to be, the Rawlsian approach would be radicalized in quite a fundamental way.

Another version of the indirect duty view was developed by Jan Narveson, who assumes that the moral community is composed of 'rational egoists' seeking to maximize their utilities, desires and wants. In order for these 'rational egoists' or fully autonomous individuals to live together, in ways which do not constantly infringe the lives and property of others, a system of moral rules emerges to regulate individual behaviour. Narveson's view of the nature of the moral community as a function of self-interest is much more disturbing for the cases for animal liberation or for animal rights. He suggests that the case for animal rights involves an 'argument from marginal cases': that, since we accord respect for humans with lower faculties than some animals, we must treat human and non-human animals alike. For Narveson, however, the position of young children or the 'mental enfeebled' is safeguarded by the presumption that human beings would want to protect their own children. All rational egoists could, with age or illness, lose the capacities which presently act as an entry ticket to the moral community (see Narveson 1977). This position is similar in some respects to that of Frey, for whom membership of the moral community (and thus recognition of others' interests) is dependent on the full exercise of rational thought, language and an awareness of one's own ethical position within this community. In this way, animals have no interests which automatically deserve recognition. But neither do human beings who do not possess these capacities. Nevertheless, the position of children and others who lack these capacities is secured through the duties of members of the moral community to act as guardians for them.

While Narveson attempts to limit the obligations of human beings to non-human animals, Stephen Clark's *The Moral Status of Animals* (1977) uses the indirect duty view to extend these obligations. Clark places the human treatment of non-human animals in the context of respect for the integrity of the 'commonwealth of the biosphere' (of all living things and their life support systems). This places both human and non-human animals as subcategories within a greater system of living things. Clark offers an account of the way in which human beings make sense of the complexity of existence, by wrapping experiences of the natural world within cultural representations. In this way, he suggests, representations of natural things mirror cultural forms rather than providing an unmediated access to the natural. The vanity or arrogance of human beings ensures that they are incapable of acknowledging the tiny niche they actually occupy within complex and incomprehensible networks of biotic relations. Clark's project is to reduce the ethical significance of the human species. In the commonwealth of the biosphere, all living things have a right to the full realization of their potentialities and capacities. The treatment of animals is a vital indicator of the relationship between human beings and nature, serving as an index of impending catastrophe. Our duties to animals are identified in an indirect way. At the centre of this argument for respecting nature and the 'unity of life', there is an appeal to the self-interest of human beings.

Regan asks us to consider both direct and indirect duty views as flawed, for they confuse the relationship between moral agency and the morality of actions. Direct duty approaches balance the infliction of pain on animals against the enjoyment (or relief of pain) of human beings. Indirect duty views, with the partial exception of Clark, regard the treatment of animals as an index of humanitarianism or view our obligations to animals in terms of a duty to human interests or a divine being. In neither case is the intrinsic or inherent value of the animals themselves considered. Regan's response is to widen the moral community by grounding it upon the equality of individuals as having value in themselves, a value which goes beyond their experiences of pleasure and pain. Conventionally, this applies only to moral agents who can fully and directly participate in the moral community. However, for Regan, this also applies to 'moral patients', that is, beings which lack some of the capacities for participating in the moral community but still deserve some consideration, by virtue of some common characteristics they hold with the moral agents. The attempt to demarcate agents and patients in terms of their value, or in terms of their total 'pleasures-over-pains', is arbitrary. As Regan states:

> Morality will not tolerate the use of double standards when cases are relevantly similar. If we postulate inherent value in the case of moral agents and recognise the need to view their possession of it as being equal, then we are rationally obliged to do the same in the case of moral patients. All who have inherent value have it equally . . . Inherent value is thus a categorical concept. One either has it, or one does not. There are no in-betweens. Moreover, all those who have it, have it equally. It does not come in degrees.
>
> (Regan 1984: 240–41)

This approach regards the identification of the intrinsic value of a being as a matter of establishing not simply whether the thing in question is alive but rather whether the living being displays the characteristics of being a 'subject of life'. This means, as indicated earlier, that in order to secure moral consideration, the being must display beliefs, desires, a sense of memory and the future, intentions, emotions, identity and an awareness of how actions are likely to affect its welfare. This would also mean that subjects of life view their own interests independently of their utility for others. If any living being demonstrates these capabilities then that being is worthy of the attribution of equal intrinsic value. This means that it must be treated with the respect accorded to all individuals. By this criterion, vegetarianism becomes an obligation of the respect which should be accorded universally and equally to all members of the moral community. As a result of attributing rights to animals, animal farming is unjust, hunting and trapping for sport or commerce are wrong, and the use of animals in education, toxicity tests and other forms of scientific research violates the intrinsic value of the animals concerned.

Animals and ecosystems

An indication of the foundational issues involved in the discussion of the relationship between human and non-human animals can be seen in the consideration of endangered species. Conventional approaches suggest that such species should be protected to maintain biodiversity and to ensure that the species is around for the benefit of future generations of human beings. Animals are therefore often seen as renewable resources and, as such, can be exploited in a way that finite resources such as fossil fuels should not. Regan, however, justifies the protection of animals simply on the grounds that they are animals and would condemn the exploitation or killing of animals regardless of the present scarcity or abundance of the animals in question. When considering ecocentric arguments, Regan questions approaches developed by writers such as Aldo Leopold who explore the place of both human and non-human animals in terms of the impact upon the biotic community as a whole. In particular, Regan disapproves of the way in which animal rights could be ignored by taking into account the 'best consequences for the community'. One of the most common justifications for the culling of a particular species is the possibility of species overpopulation damaging the ecosystem they inhabit.

Nevertheless, the recognition of the place of animals within some broader conception of the ecosystem, biotic community or 'commonwealth of living things' does not necessarily subsume the consideration of respect for animals. For a start, Regan is himself unsure about the boundary between those animals which do conform to his criterion for respect as subjects of life and those which do not. He recommends that human beings should always act cautiously when dealing with animals on the margins of this criterion. However, he does not address three features which characterize ecosystems – complexity, uncertainty and interconnectedness – and the implications they have for any clear statement of human responsibilities towards other animals, other forms of life and the conditions which make life possible. It is to these missing dimensions that we now turn.

- *Complexity*. Most human decisions are conducted in the light of available knowledge and understanding. This is likely to be flawed in two ways. First, we are often selective in terms of the manifest knowledge and evidence we consider to be relevant in any given case. Second, human beings base their decisions and actions within unacknowledged conditions, drawing upon tacit knowledge about the right course of action to take.
- *Uncertainty*. All human decisions involve elements of risk for, despite all attempts to guarantee specific outcomes, there is always the likelihood that unintended consequences will emerge which are damaging for some elements of the complex ecosystem. We should be suspicious of all attempts to search for simplicity in defining the conditions appropriate for the relationships between species and the conditions which enable them to exist.
- *Interconnectedness*. The manifest complexity and uncertainty of the natural order, which contemporary science has barely begun to acknowledge, are made even more relevant for making moral decisions when we recognize that changes in one part of the ecosystem will have implications elsewhere. When we make moral decisions which are designed to foster the potential of all humans or all animals in Regan's moral community, then we also have to recognize that we may be unleashing a whole series of alterations and changes to the ecosystem with effects counter to the original intention.

We will return to these issues in the final chapter when assessing the prospects for ecological citizenship. In particular, we should be careful to acknowledge the dangers involved in making an arbitrary distinction between animals we respect and everything else in the biotic community, especially along the lines of anthropocentric justifications of the superiority of the human species. In a complex ecosystem or biotic community, any set of moral rules must also ensure that obligations to human beings or non-human animals cannot be identified without careful consideration of the wider ecosystem. Actually, responsibilities to animals are not necessarily undermined by considering our duties towards the land, forests and woodland, the oceans, mountains and the biosphere. On these grounds, human duties and obligations should not be limited to respect for animals because they display family resemblances to the human species.

4 Ecology, Individualism and the Social Order

One of the most important areas explored in this and the next chapter is the relationship between environmental ethics and traditions within social and political thought. In this chapter, we will focus our attention upon the liberal and conservative traditions, drawing out some of the implications of the liberal ethical approaches considered in the earlier chapters. In the next chapter, we turn our attention to the relationship between ecological thought and traditions which contain projects for transformation and emancipation of various kinds, such as socialism, feminism and anarchism. In particular, the traditions considered will be evaluated for their theoretical responses to the notion of respect for nature, as well as in relation to the practical consequences upon the green environment from social systems based upon them. Some issues will bridge both chapters – in particular, the role of market systems of economic production, distribution and exchange. However, the ways in which the markets are viewed and evaluated will depend upon the particular value positions of each tradition. In this chapter, we will concentrate upon market systems characterized by the institutional feature of private property and capitalist exchange relations. In addition, more recent attempts to celebrate the positive effects of the market will be considered through an exploration of neo-liberal approaches to the relationship between capitalism and the green environment.

The approaches considered in the debates on our obligations to future generations of human beings and to non-human animals fall into two broad forms of liberal thinking. On the one hand, there are deontological approaches which emphasize the importance of establishing 'justice' through a system of rules, acting as a universally valid guide to moral action. Examples of these include the contractarian views of Rawls, Nozick and Regan considered in Chapters 2 and 3. Each offers a fundamentally different vision of the most appropriate basis for a just arrangement. However, each suggests that the most appropriate form of human order is one based upon rules which can be taken as valid and just in all circumstances. These forms of moral system are concerned with the rules within which the members of the moral community seek to further their respective goals and interests, rather than the consequences of the actions involved. Even in Regan's case, membership of the moral community carries with it the obligation to respect the intrinsic value of all members, only here the membership criterion has been broadened in order to include non-human animals as well as people.

The alternative approaches focus exclusively upon the consequences of the actions under consideration. In particular, the utilitarian version of this approach (adopted by Peter Singer) develops an account of the condition on non-human animals which only considers the balance between suffering and enjoyment of those involved. A 'just' outcome is one which serves the collective good. From the point of view of deontological approaches, actions which violate the principle of justice are universally unjust. This does not mean, however, that one understanding of justice has come to be seen as universally true, only that those who adopt a particular view of justice believe that it should be applied universally, as can be seen in the differences between Rawls and Nozick. However, in the calculations of the utilitarian approach, the level of suffering is measured against the level of enjoyment in order to achieve the largest sum of happiness. Even if an action has negative consequences for some members of a community, so long as the total outcome has greater benefits than costs, then one can say that the outcome is just. These differences in approach, and all that follows from them, run all the way throughout liberal thinking and therefore deserve careful consideration when examining the liberal approach to the natural world and the impact of human beings upon it.

Liberal thinking and the environment

Before we approach the liberal view of the green environment, it is useful to establish the broad assumptions of the liberal position. The liberal approach contains certain basic themes which are combined in different ways and with different levels of emphasis. As a starting point, it is assumed that all choices in life are (or should be) made by autonomous individuals who make decisions guided by a set of moral presuppositions. The areas of social existence seen as characterized by *individualism* are the economy, politics, intellectual enquiry and religious belief. The role of individual actors is tied to the idea of *toleration* of views or interests other than one's own. Such toleration, liberals argue, can only exist within definite rule-governed situations. This is, in turn, connected to *universalism*, the view that any such rule system must apply equally to all members of the moral community in accordance with an underlying conception of justice. Any system of rules which is adopted should be judged in terms of how it delivers the goals and supports the interests of the members of the community concerned, bearing in mind that it is impossible to specify the various and changing goals of all the members of any social order. In situations of conflict, the existence of an impartial arbiter acting as a 'known and indifferent judge' should be in place to mediate in disputes and to reconcile grievances. Generally, liberals believe that 'rule by rules' is preferable to 'rule by men', for this acts as a means of curbing arbitrary exercises of power. This is often related to the idea of *meliorism*, that human beings have the potential for improvement (if not perfection) within appropriate social conditions. Such improvements can be measured in terms of individual gains or the promotion of collective happiness. In practice, the operation of systems of rules may come into conflict with the maximization of happiness within society. The differences between these two imperatives can be seen in the difference between the Kantian and utilitarian views considered earlier.

It is worthwhile considering the sort of order which liberals see as appropriate in relation to the concerns of environmental politics. Two tendencies can be identified, which I shall label as critical and progressive liberalism. Critical liberals, by and large, tend to see the state as having definite limits but ensuring that certain basic functions are performed to protect the members of the society from each other or from other social orders. These basic functions involve the maintenance of defence and internal public order but, most importantly, the regulation of a market system based upon the principle of private ownership of property. In this tendency, there is a particular emphasis on the conditions which maximize the opportunities for individuals in competition with other members of society. This tendency operates in opposition to the beliefs of progressive liberals. Instead, the progressive view advocates benevolent state intervention directly in the private lives of the citizens of a society in order to ensure that the society progresses and the condition of its members improves over time. Progressive liberals place a special emphasis upon meliorism and draw upon utilitarian arguments that the state should seek to establish conditions for the promotion of collective happiness. Individualism is thus checked by meliorism in order to ensure that inequalities do not get out of hand and thus act as a limit on the potential for conflict.

One brief example serves to illustrate the diversity of liberal thinking and how this has implications for considering how to deal with environmental issues. One of the key concerns in recent debates, about how future forms of development can be sustainable, has been on population control. This is a typical way of addressing a qualitative problem, namely the consumption patterns of existing people, by posing a quantitative solution, through advocating a limit on future population growth. Instead of raising questions about how the densely populated societies in the West over-consume and pollute, the standard response is to leave this unchallenged and fix upon the potential for billions more people elsewhere, in developing societies, doing the same. The answer proposed has been birth control in various forms. However, this raises new dilemmas for liberals. For instance, voluntary projects focusing on sex education and birth control have only been partially successful. Cultural values concerning reproduction as well as economic imperatives continue to encourage high levels of fertility in many developing societies.

Population growth on a large scale over a relatively short period of time is a typical feature in the demographic transition which accompanies economic development. As mortality declines, without a corresponding decrease in birth rates, population levels tend to increase rapidly. The usual outcome is the limitation of birth rates, so that families can enjoy the benefits of a higher material standard of living and invest more in a limited number of children.

Empirical evidence suggests that during the most important phase in which fertility declined in the UK, from the late nineteenth to mid-twentieth centuries, the most prominent reason was abstinence from sex rather than from technological forms of contraception (Gittens 1982). This suggests that the transition is culturally shaped rather than following a definite plan, and is hence open to significant variation. Western societies have stabilized with lower levels of mortality but correspondingly lower levels of fertility. Western governments, and the international bodies they dominate, tend to view population control from this standpoint.

Liberals are faced with a choice of whether to advocate compulsory population control (such as sterilization without consent) or live with the consequences of a larger human population, with all of its consequent increases in the demand for resources and the production of human waste. Societies with severe measures for 'excessive reproduction', such as China, are often regarded as intolerant and authoritarian for infringing personal freedom. Nevertheless, the introduction of penalties or the loss of privileges for exceeding a family reproduction quota can be justified within the utilitarian framework, if it can be demonstrated that the pain suffered by those who violate reproduction norms is more than offset by the benefits enjoyed throughout this society. In the case of China, with a population in excess of one billion and limited arable land space, the measures have been seen as essential for avoiding starvation as much as for ensuring benefits more generally. John Passmore (1974) has suggested that while compulsory sterilization is a violation of individual rights, punishing someone for exceeding a general legislative rule on excessive reproduction is not a violation. Of course, such general reproduction rules must be the product of a process of democratic deliberation (rather than imposed arbitrarily) and the enforcement of these rules must be subject to due process and offer grounds for appeal. This does not take us away from the problem that, in practice, such measures are more likely to have an impact upon societies which are presently undergoing the demographic transition towards becoming developed societies. In Western societies, with low fertility and stability in population size today, such measures were never put into operation during their own demographic transition.

Despite these differences, all liberals are keen to stress the importance of the distinction between the state and civil society.

This is sometimes characterized as the distinction between the *public* domain of parliamentary and administrative institutions and the *private* domain where the existence of free choices is seen as the litmus test of a liberal social order. Liberals have very different views as to where the precise boundary between private and public should actually lie. Nevertheless, they are all convinced of the importance of the distinction itself. Ecological thinking poses significant difficulties for liberals because of the way it challenges the very existence of this distinction. Concern with the environment immediately raises the possibility of interfering with private choices. In particular, recent concerns about consumption patterns in relation to the environment have prompted consumers to make ethical decisions when purchasing a particular range of goods and services. Some high-profile campaigns have led consumers to avoid goods and services which damage the environment in particular ways. Consumers have boycotted tins of tuna from Pacific fishing fleets using 'wall of death' fishing nets, deodorant sprays which contain chemicals which damage the ozone layer and cosmetics which involve animal testing. In this way, individuals have been persuaded to make such choices, although they are also free to ignore such appeals. When the instructions to change private choices emerge from state authorities, the implications are somewhat different. For instance, in the area of transport policy, it is feasible that in the near future freedom of mobility will be much more closely regulated in order to discourage car use and encourage changes in employment practices, such as working from home.

Most Western societies rely very heavily on car use as a means of transportation, and this reliance is growing with the emergence of two-car households, in addition to the increased transportation of freight by road. This has generated a range of problems such as air pollution and traffic congestion. The average speed of traffic in London in 1996 was 11 miles (18 kilometres) per hour, the same as by horse and cart in 1896. The expansion of highway construction and the erosion of alternative transport facilities throughout the twentieth century have merely promoted further car use, rather than resolving the problems involved. This means that state authorities will increasingly intervene in private transport choices in order to deal with the problem of 'gridlock' in the areas of greatest transport congestion. This could take the form of highway tolls, restriction of use to alternate days, car-free zones, higher road taxation and the fining of drivers in cars without passengers. All these are curative measures, for they respond to a problem after it has already become intolerable. Preventive measures raise questions which many feel unhappy dealing with, the most basic being whether we should travel so much in the first place. Western economies have become increasingly dependent upon the workforce travelling long distances, and long-range commuting has been one of the most significant new developments in work patterns in the late twentieth century. New microelectronic communications, combined with the carrying capacity of fibre-optic cables, allow for an efficient dialogue between individuals in different places. This development may provide a sort of answer for those who can work and communicate through email and video-conferencing. Even in organizations which rely upon electronic communication, small face-to-face groups continue to be seen as much more productive in solving problems and developing innovation. Most forms of work still cannot yet use technology in this way. Short of placing a statutory limit on the distance which any individual travels to work, which liberals would regard as a gross infringement of freedom of mobility, some form of co-ordinated transport policy provides a viable working alternative.

State involvement through the management and regulation of transport seems to offer a short-term stopgap to ensure that large numbers of individuals travel cost-effectively in a coordinated fashion, rather than add to road congestion. State involvement through public ownership and the subsidization of private companies, for the maintenance of unprofitable transport routes, serves to ensure that mass transportation is a little less wasteful. Even a bus or train which is half full uses less energy than if all the passengers travelled by car. If we examine this kind of public involvement in private relationships, we can identify a number of ways of justifying state intervention by reference to liberal values and assumptions. For a start, public ownership and subsidy can be justified by reference to collective welfare. The happiness of all is best served by the provision of a variety of means of transport, even if this means that some, such as car users, have to pay additional taxes. This conforms to the utilitarian principle that aggregate costs can be offset by benefits elsewhere. Alternatively, state inducements can be used as a way of prompting changes in the behaviour of individuals making self-interested decisions. An example of this is the use of the taxation system to ensure that lead-free petrol is consistently cheaper than other forms of fuel. This leaves the decision with the individual and does not involve coercion from a state authority. By creating a situation in which rational individuals are willing to invest in engine modifications to their private vehicles to benefit from cheaper fuel, such a strategy also leads to lower levels of lead pollution.

On the one hand, utilitarian liberals can justify state intervention in situations where the losses of some would be offset against the gains elsewhere. On the other hand, liberal contractarians offer a model which allows for the persuasion of individuals to behave differently out of conscience or self-interest but which does not violate the right of individuals to behave how they choose. In each case, it should be stressed, the measure against which all decisions are compared is the extent to which such changes affect human beings. Measures which attempt to change human behaviour merely moderate the problem, for many of the restraints on human activity that ecologism proposes may harm the interests of human beings or violate their right to act otherwise. Liberal thought does not involve the recognition of obligations to things other than human beings. Ecological thinking does not sit easily in a liberal framework, based upon either of the sets of assumptions identified, and it raises problems with values and assumptions in liberal thinking from top to bottom. Nevertheless, there is some mileage in exploring how far we can go towards an environmental ethic within the liberal framework.

Neo-liberal thinking and the environment

To begin, it is worth exploring how contemporary critical liberals – that is, the advocates of neo-liberalism – have addressed these issues, particularly since they have been influential in shaping policy-making in the United Kingdom and the United States during the 1980s. Neo-liberal attitudes towards the environment are informed by Lockean conceptions of private property mediated through the individualistic approach of Nozick. In effect, neo-liberalism celebrates the operation of capitalist market systems where individuals, households and companies engage in competition and cooperation in order to ensure the benefits of material progress. A good example of this approach can be seen in the work of Peter Saunders, as the following extract indicates:

> Capitalism, we have seen, is a growth machine. Competition between capitalist producers stimulates perpetual innovation. The result is that basic resources such as food and clothing come to be produced in ever greater quantities at ever reduced costs while new luxury items become commonplace within the space of a generation. Average living standards are thus perpetually transformed. Across the world, per capita incomes rise even as total populations expand. It is as if we have come into possession of the alchemists' secret of how to turn base metal into gold.
>
> (Saunders 1995: 52)

Saunders engages directly with the green critique of 'growth mania' within the capitalist way of life and within industrial societies generally. He attempts to demonstrate the affinities between some strands of ecological thought and socialist strategies for regulating and interfering in private choices. He notes, with irony, that just as capitalism demonstrates that it can deliver a good life for most if not all members of the societies which embrace it, so capitalism has now been condemned for its success. Growth poses significant difficulties in terms of the capacity of the ecosystem to provide enough in the way of natural resources for satisfying human aspirations, as well as being able to cope with the wastes created by human economic activities. Saunders acknowledges these concerns but raises doubts about the possible apocalyptic consequences posed by some green activists. He highlights some of the implications of population control measures for individual freedom, in this case, the freedom to reproduce. Saunders highlights the tendency of greens 'to control, regulate, limit, ban or even reverse the technological development which has made economic growth possible in the past' (ibid.: 54). He proposes an alternative attitude to the problems involved in environmental change and damage posed by global capitalist economic growth. He argues that attempts to limit resource extraction, pollution and population growth create their own costs. All regulation, he suggests, even bans, will impose significant costs, whether this involves the application of technological devices to existing productive processes or surveillance of human activities.

Adopting a cost–benefit framework, Saunders suggests that the costs of cleaning up one form of productive activity could have more beneficial consequences if they were redeployed in other productive ways. If developing societies, which now provide the heavy industrial production of the global economy, find themselves coping with most of the costs without enjoying many of the benefits of global growth patterns, then this is even more unfair. In addition, he suggests, prophecies of doom have been misplaced in the past for they take no account of the dynamic tendencies of capitalist markets. Of particular importance is the capacity of capitalist enterprises to discover new ways of identifying and extracting natural resources as well as using technological innovation to increase the efficiency of human machines and reduce the problems of pollution. Market forces are seen as a vital motivating factor in seeking out ways of doing things which mitigate some of the damaging effects of capitalism even though these developments are unplanned. For Saunders, the existence of a technofix culture means that 'the more prosperous capitalist countries become, the more "environmentally friendly" their industries' (ibid.: 65).

A substantial foundation of the argument developed by Peter Saunders is drawn from the thought experiments of Garrett Hardin. This approach involves the use of game theory in order to consider the role of the systems of private property on the natural environment and the implications of liberal thinking on personal freedom. Hardin starts out from the assumption that all individuals are rational choice 'minimaxers', that is, we decide to act on the basis of calculating what likely outcome will maximize our benefits and minimize our costs. He poses a very effective scenario or game in which all the players are herdsmen living off the same limited common land. Rational herdsmen, who perceive no limit to the carrying capacity of the land, persistently add to their respective herds of animals to the point that the common land is exhausted. For Hardin, the 'tragedy of the commons' means that:

> Each man is locked into a system that compels him to increase his herd without limit – in a world that is limited. Ruin is the destination to which all men rush, each pursuing his own best interest in a society that believes in the freedom of the commons. Freedom in a commons brings ruin to all.
>
> (Hardin 1993: 132)

The answer to the tragedy of the commons, according to Hardin, is the development of definite relations of ownership, either in private or public hands, in order to ration the use of natural resources. In private hands, it is often argued, land is maintained in the long-term interests of the owners and of successive generations. This can be seen in family holdings of forestry lands, where the financial return from replanting trees in the space where trees have been recently felled may be one or two generations away. In public ownership, the uses of national park facilities have been limited to prevent overuse. Hardin suggests that while these are not perfect ways to resolve the problem, they are still necessary. Saunders does not consider this range of possibilities in his reading of Hardin and focuses upon the situations where ownership is more problematic, such as fishing in an open sea or polluting a shared atmosphere. In these cases, the tragedy of the commons is a distinct possibility, although 'fouling one's own nest' replaces 'overgrazing' as the mechanism of ecological destruction. Hardin's response is to raise questions about the 'freedom to breed'. Pollution is seen as a direct consequence of too many people all wishing to have a high standard of living. This sort of infringement on individual liberty is viewed by Saunders as a sign of the dangers of much of green thought. From the neo-liberal standpoint, in green plans for transformation, freedom is often sacrificed in the name of the greater good. Members of society are therefore coerced into behaving in ways that ecological activists approve and demand.

As an alternative to this tendency to turn to coercion as the answer, Saunders proposes the commodification process as an answer. At this point, he introduces the argument about property ownership developed by Hardin in order to augment his case, even though he disagrees with Hardin's general conclusions. For instance, Saunders suggests that endangered species would be better served if local populations were allowed to use them for commercial purposes. In particular, he raises concrete evidence, from Zimbabwe, on the way in which ivory poaching is best overcome if local people have an interest in preventing outside poachers from undermining their own interests. In this way, it is even possible to think of the conservation of endangered species through commercial means such as 'rhino-burgers' and 'giraffe-U-like'. In this 'fast-food' approach to species conservation, even endangered animal species come to be seen as a renewable natural resource for human use. Of course, such solutions do not address the conditions of life of these animals in captivity, nor do they resolve the issues raised about the importance of the maintenance of natural habitats with considerable biodiversity.

This leads to another related question – what solutions to environmental problems are feasible in a free market? Besides the privatization of public goods such as endangered species, Saunders highlights the role of green consumerism and charging for common resources. The marketing of goods and services as 'environmentally friendly' or 'ethically sound' is a significant feature of contemporary advertising and has been known to redirect purchasing power away from forms of production which are perceived to damage the environment. However, without perfect information about how goods are produced and a willingness to accept higher prices, at least in the short term, this is unlikely to achieve fundamental shifts in economic activity. As indicated in the example earlier, on lead-free petrol, one way in which to encourage changes in the way in which people behave, without coercion, is to offer inducements such as tax breaks. Alternatively, firms or agricultural enterprises can pay to pollute, encouraging companies to invest in more effective waste disposal systems in order to cut costs. Although this has encouraged some reductions in waste as well as contributing directly to clean-up costs, it does not offer much of an incentive to many significant high polluters where the cost of changing the production process exceeds the cost of paying for waste discharge. The emergence of 'pollution permit' trading enables firms which reduce their waste output to sell their pollution permits to other firms who are exceeding their waste allowances. This means that firms receive a reduction in costs by being efficient in their use of resources and by introducing waste reduction systems. However, firms which continue to pollute face additional costs. Similar trading relationships have been established as a way of conserving fish stocks through the introduction of 'fishing quotas'. All such systems have loopholes but they do serve to place total limits on both the extraction of natural resources and pollution levels. However, they do not require the participants to act in particular ways, they merely offer incentives to do so. For Saunders, this avoids the problems of coercion.

Conservative thinking and the environment

An alternative to the dominance of neo-liberal approaches towards the environment on the right of the political spectrum has surfaced in recent conservative thinking. Many conservative philosophers and social and political theorists have expressed concern at the dominance of free market ideas in the governments and political parties of the right. The deregulation of many aspects of society in the name of individualism produced a considerable backlash from conservatives who were concerned with the moral fabric. In particular, they emphasized the loss of community, the collapse of the 'small platoons' (voluntary associations) which mediated between state and family and the decline of moral standards as acquisitiveness came to replace the sense of duty and responsibility which they believed held society together.

In the UK, the prime minister during the 1980s, Margaret Thatcher, uttered the words 'There is no such thing as society' with the intention, no doubt, of highlighting the view that individuals should not look to the state to resolve all their personal difficulties. However, for the conservative tradition, this served as an indication of the collapse of social responsibility and the dawn of a hedonistic society engaged in unrestrained wish fulfilment rather than sensible moderation. There has been a tendency to associate ecological thought and green politics with socialist movements rather than considering the conservative view of nature as a powerful vision of how to live in harmony with the natural world. Conservatives intuitively combine a respect for nature with a belief in the virtues of private property. Unlike neo-liberal thinking, which sees natural things as simply exploitable, for conservatives natural things are part of a complex web of life of which human beings are just one significant part.

One of the most eloquent outlines and defences of the conservative position on the green environment and the relationship between natural things and human beings can be seen in John Gray's essay 'An Agenda for Green Conservatism'. In particular, Gray reproaches right-minded thinkers for leaving green political issues in the hands of the left. Traditional conservative virtues and beliefs, he suggests, are much more in tune with green theory than socialist, anarchist and feminist politics. Ecological thought seems to spend too much time criticizing capitalist markets and turning a blind eye to the environmental consequences of state planning. He characterizes neo-liberals as 'secular liberal utopians' engaged in rationalist experimentation with the principles of government and society. Human beings, he argues, need more than liberty, they need 'a home, a network of common practices and inherited traditions that confers on them the blessing of a settled identity' (Gray 1993: 125).

In order to substantiate his critique of liberal thinking, Gray rejects the idea of seeing the human condition as constituted by *rational individual decision makers* divorced from space and time. The existence of a web of relationships and, with that, the maintenance of a suitable natural environment, are considered to be as vital to human flourishing as bread and water. Gray's counterblast is so strongly put because he feels that this has been lost in conservative politics in recent years. For Gray, market institutions are indispensable but they are not in themselves sufficient for maintaining an adequate environment. He draws similar lessons to Peter Saunders from Hardin's 'tragedy of the commons' on the role of private property in ensuring that over-exploitation does not take place. Gray also adds that the price mechanism is a crucially important way of highlighting resource scarcity. The market and associated relations of private property are, therefore, necessary for conservation but, unlike the neo-liberal view, he argues that they are not sufficient for a harmonious relationship with natural things. Markets are geared towards a permanent state of economic growth and involve a myriad of small acts which, in their aggregation, can have enormous implications, such as global warming. The logic of the market involves the assumption that the many small self-interested actions of individuals will have the consequence of benefiting everyone to some extent. It does not allow for ecological catastrophe, and no amount of market pricing to encourage efficient use of resources will prevent unanticipated consequences such as these. Markets on a global scale are also damaging to local economies and local cultures and, in turn, the traditions which have been transmitted across generations. Markets can undermine the complex and unplanned accumulation of practices which bind communities and societies together.

Gray provides a useful account of the ways in which conservative values and assumptions converge with ecological thought, affinities which set them both apart from other political ideologies or movements. First, Gray draws upon the ideas of conservative philosophy, expressed by Edmund Burke two centuries ago, on the need for a partnership between past, present and future generations. Both conservative and ecological thought raise the importance of a 'multi-generational perspective' rather than the one-generational contract (perhaps including their children) with strangers which tends to predominate in liberal thought. He argues that a fixation on the present, rather than on what we do for posterity, is a recipe for exploitation and waste rather than careful husbandry and guardianship. In this sense, conservatism provides an important example of intergenerational justice, by recognizing that future generations should be accounted for in present decisions. Second, Gray highlights the stress on common social relations in conservative and ecological thought. The celebration of free choice in recent liberal and conservative thinking becomes the target in this comment.

> For conservatives, as for green thinkers, it is clear that choice-making has in itself little or no value . . . The ultimate locus of value in the human world is not therefore in individual choices but in forms of life. This should leave us to qualify, even to abandon, the ideal of the autonomous chooser (which I have myself elsewhere endorsed) in favour of the recognition that the good life for human beings – as for many kindred animal species – necessarily presupposes embeddedness in communities.
>
> (Gray 1993: 137)

Gray concludes that the tendency to extend liberal conceptions of rights to non-human animals is an inappropriate development, for rights are social rather than abstract things. For Gray, it is 'forms of life', both social and natural, that need to be protected, not individual rights. Third, there is an affinity of attitude between ecological thinkers and conservative philosophers, for both are prone to 'risk-aversion'. For conservative theorists, *prudence* is the key virtue in dealing with a complex and unpredictable matter such as the relationship between society and nature. In this sense, both emphasize practical strategies which have been established through trial and error, rather than bold new plans for innovation. This draws out one of the most important characteristics of ecological thinking. Despite the rhetorical calls for change, transformation and a dismantling of human practices which damage the environment, the alternatives proposed are small-scale, localized economies and societies based upon past practices which could exist in some degree of harmony with the ecosystems they inhabit.

Contemporary industrial production and agricultural techniques all involve intervening in natural processes which affect ecosystems in fairly substantive ways. Many of these interventions have unpredictable outcomes and entail a significant risk of adverse consequences. For this reason the principle which should replace growth is stability. A conservative vision of change is one which emphasizes evolutionary growth, whereby social relationships become more complex and differentiated but nevertheless more interdependent. The use of the organic analogy is a key feature of the conservative account of social relations and processes. When considering human decisions in relationship to change, conservatives recommend that we should adopt the attitude of prudent gardeners rather than tearing everything up by the roots and starting again. By making a virtue of the promotion of stability, Gray is able to draw upon the idea of the 'steady-state economy' developed by John Stuart Mill, on the grounds that it captures the core of the argument for sustainable development. Both conservative and ecological thought try to break the relationship between the belief in infinite growth (alongside other variants of the language of 'never ending progress') and the conditions for human flourishing. Both believe that we shall reach a point where we have to think imaginatively with what we have.

One moral system or many?

Finally, in this chapter, we need to reassess the potential of liberal thinking in relation to ecological concerns as well as the problems within it. Liberal thinking on rights has been utilized creatively to question the anthropocentric assumptions which underpin liberal ethics. If we accept that rights or entitlements (and the associated duties or obligations) do not end at the species barrier between human beings and other things, then the idea of the 'moral community' at the heart of liberal thinking is transformed. We have already encountered one attempt to do this in Chapter 3, in the case for animal rights developed by Tom Regan. For animal rights to exist, he argued, the intrinsic value of non-human animals had to be recognized and acted upon. All animals were seen as 'ends in themselves' rather than a means to some other (human) end. Christopher D. Stone has also considered whether this kind of argument can be developed to transform the ethical status of trees. In his seminal article, 'Should Trees Have Standing' (1972), Stone was responding to a particular legal case where the limits of the liberal approach to the moral and legal standing of natural things were being stretched. For Stone, the history of the relationship between legal systems and ethical debates has demonstrated that the attribution of rights is by no means fixed and has been constantly open to challenge.

Stone highlights the case of the legal dispute of *Sierra Club* v. *Morton*, where the development of a project to build a ski resort in the Mineral King Valley of Sequoia National Forest prompted a case which went as far as the Supreme Court. The environmentalist organization, the Sierra Club, sought to demonstrate that the trees which inhabited the area had legal standing. Its case rested on the argument that the trees could be taken as persons suffering a 'legal wrong' as a result of being adversely affected by some action. In this case, the Sierra Club attempted to assert that the trees on the site in question would be adversely affected by the development and, on their behalf, filed a suit against the Secretary of the Interior, Morton, who had authorized the development of the location by the Walt Disney Corporation. Stone's case for considering the 'rights of rightless things' offers a basis for rethinking our relationship with natural things:

> The fact is that each time there is a movement to confer rights onto some new 'entity', the proposal is bound to sound odd or frightening or laughable. This is partly because until the rightless thing receives its rights, we cannot see it as anything but as a thing for the use of 'us' – those who are holding rights at this time.
>
> (Stone 1972: 455)

Stone argues that the legal system already recognizes a whole range of things as persons for legal purposes which are not really persons in the conventional sense, such as banks and corporations. On this basis, the exclusion of trees is an arbitrary decision in much the same way as human beings themselves have often been denied legal standing. However, the Supreme Court majority judgement rejected this legal initiative, on the grounds that a legal person would be able to demonstrate that suffering and injury had taken or would take place. The trees, as the petitioner, could not demonstrate 'individualized harm' and therefore lacked standing. Since this case, Stone argues, a river, a marsh, a brook, a commons, a species of rare bird, a national monument (Death Valley) and an anonymous tree have all petitioned as 'persons' in legal disputes, with little in the way of a significant result. In one case, an individual who released two dolphins constructed a defence on the basis of setting such 'persons' free from captivity. However, the court ruled that dolphins were not persons and, therefore, the defendant lost the case. Clearly, trees, lakes or dolphins cannot represent themselves in court, and as such cannot have legal standing in the terms of reference of the law as it stands.

Stone became frustrated with the idea that we somehow had to choose between a deontological or utilitarian framework to resolve these problems. In particular, he questioned the tendency of moral philosophy to pose the existence of one moral answer to all questions. Rather than choosing between them, in *Earth and Other Ethics* (1987) he recommends the adoption of moral pluralism. Stone advocates the attribution of moral standpoints according to definite spheres of existence, rather than suggesting that one form of morality is applicable across all forms of existence. For Stone, this means that our attitudes towards natural things differ from the moral relations between fully fledged members of the moral community. Trees would have legal standing through the agency of persons acting as guardians on their behalf. This would give trees the same position as children or humans in a 'persistent vegetative state'. In the legal dispute in which Stone was engaged, then the Sierra Club would act as the legal guardian for the trees in Mineral King Valley.

In many respects this is similar to the line of argument developed by Tom Regan on the difference between moral agents and moral patients – that agents can and should act on behalf of patients in situations where the moral patients are clearly unable to act on their own behalf. Of course, moral status cannot necessarily be attributed to non-human things on the basis that they are subjects of life in the sense developed by animal rights campaigners. Legal considerability has already been attributed to non-human things such as lakes, forests and the sea-bed but only when considering the effects of pollution in relation to their consequences for human beings. This ties legal and moral consideration purely to situations where human interests are at stake. For Stone, this cannot be the limit for ethical consideration, as his defence of trees indicates. Nevertheless, he does not believe that one moral system fits all situations. This means that we no longer have to engage in a search for the perfect moral system in order to define obligations to persons, future generations, indigenous tribes in the Amazon, transnational corporate entities, animals, species, habitats and other ecological systems. However, we then have to find a means of classifying different situations in terms of the moral reference map appropriate to the situation in question.

This shifts the focus of moral governance from the application of principles to the application of moral frameworks. For instance, Stone suggests that the ethical act of becoming a vegetarian does not follow from the application of a single principle but only makes sense when it is part of an integrated 'network of mutually supportive principles, theories, and attitudes toward consequences' (Stone 1987: 242). The moral systems so far discussed, such as utilitarianism and Kantian deontology, are transformed into competing frameworks, alongside alternative moral frameworks which place ecosystems at the centre of moral consideration, offering guidance on particular problems rather than offering absolute solutions. On these grounds it is possible to justify 'respect for persons', using a deontological framework for moral questions about human beings, but apply utilitarianism to the treatment of animals, as Nozick has suggested. However, for Nozick, human needs are clearly at the centre of any moral system. In order to explain the way in which human beings make moral choices, Stone considers the role of intuition and imagination. He suggests that moral principles are founded upon intuition, for otherwise we would not feel secure that we have made the correct moral decisions for the situation or dilemma in question. If this were not the case, we would be tortured by self-doubt and unease. However, intuitions do not stand still, for they have the capacity for development. This means that intuitions have to be thought of as open to imaginative reconstruction. If this had not occurred in the past, then respect for persons would have been limited to a few Western men, who by virtue of birth could claim both moral and legal consideration.

The case for moral pluralism is a lesson drawn from the human experience of living through a succession of moral frameworks, all of which have involved claims to be universally applicable. Moral frameworks are thus forms of situated knowledge in that they are situated in particular historical and cultural locations. We should be more careful about attributing universal claims to any system of moral guidance. If we are to take the existence of unconventional moral clients such as trees, mountains and species seriously, then we must be willing to question what moral systems are for. The liberal approach can take us a considerable way towards thinking through the status of non-human animals or other natural things. Nevertheless, there are considerable limits on how far this can be pursued. On the one hand, the universalistic claims of liberalism are open to question while, on the other, liberalism contains an underlying anthropocentrism which is, in practice, difficult to reconcile with respect for non-human things. Conservative values and assumptions demonstrate how it is possible to develop very effective forms of moral governance without endowing them with universal pretensions. Conservative morality does, after all, openly acknowledge its status as a form of situated knowledge. This does not mean that one should adopt conservatism in order to identify ecological insights, but it does demonstrate that the development of new moral systems based upon ecological assumptions is not as 'off the wall' or as 'unhinged' as has often been described. In its favour, however, conservative thinking is clearly aware of the importance of acknowledging complexity, risk and uncertainty in a way which is neglected in other political ideologies.

5 The Environment and Human Emancipation

In this chapter, we turn to the area most explored by ecological thinkers, the relationship between the recognition that human impacts upon the environment should be taken seriously and the construction of political projects for human emancipation. In the following sections, we will consider the ways in which the strategies of socialism, Marxism, anarchism and feminism have all become entangled in ecological thought. In particular, we will consider what ecological thought has drawn from these ideological movements and what they have rejected. Green politics has often concentrated its fire power on the dangers of capitalist relations of production and, consequently, has come into close contact with socialist and various radical movements. In this chapter, we will consider the connections between ecological thought and different forms of socialism, as well as radical approaches to political relations which place greater emphasis upon the need for political than for economic transformation. Despite the identification of a common foe, the transnational capitalist corporation, there is still an underlying materialism in left approaches which poses substantial difficulties for integrating ecological and socialist thought. In the wide range of socialist perspectives, materialism takes a number of forms. For instance, in social democratic accounts it is believed that the primary goal of egalitarian social reform and redistribution of wealth will deliver improvements in the standard of living. Marxists, however, take the organization of production as the starting point of any analysis of social structures and processes. These different starting points produce very different ways of thinking about social change. In turn, they have different implications for ecological thought.

Socialism and the environment

The predominant form of socialist thinking in the Western world can be described as social democracy. While this tradition has evolved in different ways in different societies, two strands of opinion within social democracy can be identified as relevant to ecological thought and its concerns. Social democracy above all is concerned with developing human progress, in both its material and moral dimensions. Each of these strands places a special emphasis upon the role of authoritative institutions engaged as benevolent actors in society, whether it be the modern welfare state or the institutions of civil society. Material progress is secured by the maintenance of economic growth, whereas moral progress is achieved by fostering duty and obligation within the social order.

In the immediate post-war phase of social democracy implemented by the Labour Party in the United Kingdom, the march of progress was achieved through modernization and technocratic management of the economy. It was believed that modernization of the economy could be achieved through the incorporation of economic interests within the policy-making process. In this way, a national plan would emerge in order to resolve the problems of a stagnant economy, with the state coordinating the representatives of capital and labour to achieve the objectives and targets established. Typically, this involved a boost to the economy through state expenditure on large-scale public works and/or private consumption through tax cuts. Success would be measured in terms of how much more was manufactured and consumed. The promotion of growth would increase the revenues available to the state, which would then be redistributed to the least well-off to make society more equal. There are some remarkable parallels between this economic strategy and the philosophical approach developed by John Rawls, leading social democrats to appropriate his account of justice to lend philosophical weight to their political programme. According to Rawls's account of the 'difference principle', the broad commitment to an egalitarian society should be moderated by the need for economic incentives. However, the inequalities which follow from the pursuit of self-interest are only permissible if they benefit those at the bottom of the social hierarchy. In real terms, this means that only through growth will poverty, squalor and ill health be ameliorated. This instrumental attitude towards natural things left little room for concern about the environment.

The modernization project, with its central political message of material growth and the redistribution of wealth, predominated in Labour Party thinking until the 1980s. However, with recent changes in the global economy, national strategies have become less relevant and effective, so that many social democratic movements have conceded ideological ground to the low taxation, free market and low public spending agenda of neo-liberalism. In this way, the state is now increasingly seen as a facilitator rather than as an organizer of the economy. As a result, in recent years, social democrats have returned to the themes of ethical socialism apparent in the labour movement in the early years of the twentieth century. This concern with 'community' and the moral fabric of society, that the social order should be the (idealized) family writ large, was always a key theme of the social democratic vision. Indeed, the state was often portrayed as a benevolent paternal figure. However, the collapse of the post-war economic boom and the failure of state planning in industrial relations, welfare, housing and so on, has prompted the social democratic movement in Britain to shift its emphasis to ethical concerns and the quality of life for all members of society. This has opened an opportunity for ecological concerns to move up the social democratic political agenda, although this remains solely for the benefit of human welfare.

Ethical socialists place a strong emphasis upon personal morality rather than grand plans and visions. In part, this draws upon the Christian socialist ethics which has played a large part in campaigns for human rights and other humanitarian causes such as the peace movement, anti-nuclear and environmental campaigns. Such concerns have occupied a central place in left-of-centre political parties in western Europe and in North America throughout the twentieth century. In short, ethical socialism places the onus of moral responsibility on states, organizations, business corporations and individuals to make the 'right choices' on investment strategies, trade contracts and personal consumption. By placing this special emphasis upon the practical considerations of making difficult moral choices, it is argued, we can think through how our decisions have definite consequences in definite circumstances. For example, a decision to invest in a small company in Tanzania which is practising and promoting sustainable development would be considered to be a better moral choice than investing in a company which disposes of untreated toxic waste into the water supply without regard for the consequences of its actions for the people in the locality. The emergence of ethical investment services within the stock market suggests a growing concern with the environmental consequences of profitable investments. The same concerns often arise in decision-making within nation-states and at other levels of administrative authority. For instance, Western governments have sometimes linked the licensing of arms exports to the human rights records of the governments which wish to purchase military hardware.

One of the most explicit attempts to develop an understanding of environmental issues and policy-making combined with a socialist ethic can be seen in Ann Taylor's *Choosing Our Future* (1992). Taylor draws upon a long history of environmental concern in the UK labour movement, which has been developed through an alliance of cooperative socialists and Nonconformist Christians. She argues that this tradition can act as a solid basis for developing a 'practical politics of the environment'. In particular, the importance of the global dimensions of environmental problems led her to conclude that only socialism had the appropriate internationalist perspective to overcome the national and regional differences which tend to block environmental initiatives. Socialism, she suggests, by emphasizing the importance of equality across national frontiers, extends the idea of community to overcome global inequalities. Nevertheless, Taylor places human needs and welfare at the centre of her analysis.

> On an emotional and intuitive level, then, the labour movement has always taken the future seriously; and in this sense it is well attuned to respond to the new threat posed by environmental degradation, which is in great measure a threat to the future. But there is also a further and more direct way in which 'environmental awareness' has long been embedded in socialist and labour movement campaigns to improve living and working conditions, through concern for the health of the working population. . . . In aspiring and organising to overcome squalor, working class people in the early labour movement were making a perfectly clear statement about the kind of environment they wanted to live in; and if this doesn't seem much like a modern 'green' concern it should be set against the equally legitimate aspirations of the two-thirds of the world's present population who still don't have

> access to adequate water and sanitation facilities. . . . The campaigns of the labour movement for medical provision, decent housing and services were, in this sense, all campaigns for a better environment.
> (Taylor 1992: 23–4)

The political language here is one of health and safety, a discourse which brings together the concerns with human welfare (conquering the five giant evils of squalor, disease, want, ignorance and idleness) with an environmental politics which considers the impact of present decisions on future generations. The elimination of poverty is seen as central to resolving environmental problems. Taylor suggests that a 'cleaner, safer and healthier environment' will be the logical consequence of taking communities more seriously. A particular emphasis is made on the coordination of legislative measures (such as planning and anti-pollution legislation) and practical local initiatives (ranging from recycling projects to the seizure of wasteland by the 'Land is Ours' campaign) as the only way to maintain environmental quality. Both Ann Taylor and Robin Cook (later to become key members of the Blair administration in the UK in 1997) have consistently campaigned since the 1970s for a special emphasis upon environmental conditions. The emphasis on 'quality of growth' rather than quantity of material assets, proposed by Cook in the 1980s, represents a new departure. Cook's appointment as Foreign Secretary in 1997 led to adoption of an 'ethical foreign policy' when dealing with issues such as human rights and environmental issues.

Socialist ethics acknowledges human-centredness as its starting point but acts as a reminder to socialists that they should not ignore the flaws of the technocratic vision of the socialist transformation. By introducing the moral dimension into discussions about human impacts upon the environment, they highlight the risks involved in policy-making. In addition, whereas the technocratic approach is run from the top by scientific experts, bureaucratic administrators and professional politicians, this second strand offers a less centralist route by emphasizing grass-roots campaigns and local control of the environment. The inspiration for this approach runs deep in the labour movement and carries with it elements of the vision of the semi-rural idyll of William Morris, in the late nineteenth century, the self-help ideals of Fabian Society pamphlets such as *Allotments and How to Get One,* and the garden-city and town planning movement founded by Ebenezer Howard. The vision of a society operating through the principle of useful work rather than useless toil is an inherent part of socialist ethics; however, it is still one where nature is valued for the instrumental uses of human beings. Despite these differences, both strands of social democratic thinking bring together a concern for social justice with the need for a healthy and safe environment in which all members of society can prosper.

Marxism and the environment

In some respects, Marx's materialist method paved the way for a recognition of the importance of ecological thought. In particular, his account of social life, as made up of relations and processes, rather than the mechanical operation of discrete things, has many affinities with ecological thought. Marxism offers an account of social life with creative human beings as the central figure. Societies are made and as such can be transformed. For Marx, it is labour power which produces value and it is the organization of work as a transformative process (transforming natural things into human-made things) which makes each mode of production so distinctive. Therefore, it is the relations and forces characterizing the economy which, in various ways, manifest themselves in the other regions of social existence. In short, it is assumed that the mode of material production shapes the social forms of the political institutions of the state, the legal system, cultural institutions, the family and community organizations and so on. Marx assumes that natural things have no value except in so far as they have been transformed in production and put to some use by human beings. One would not expect that an approach which starts from such an anthropocentric foundation would serve as fertile territory for ecological insights. However, the ongoing debate between socialist and ecological thought, between red and green perspectives, has been a significant focal point for ecological discussions in the late twentieth century.

Actually, what Marx understood precisely by the relationship between society and nature is a matter of intense dispute. For many Marxists it is common to see nature as reducible to social forms. More recently, neo-Marxists, such as Ted Benton (1989), suggest that Marx did not adequately account for natural limits on production in the light of what we now know. John Clark (1989) has drawn attention to the complexity of Marx's thinking on this issue by highlighting the way in which Marx considered nature in his early writings. In the *Economic and Philosophic Manuscripts of 1844*, Marx (1977) considers nature as the 'inorganic body' of man which becomes part of the 'organic body' through the transformative process of work, involving the appropriation of natural things. Howard Parsons, in *Marx and Engels on Ecology* (1977), raises the possibility that Marxism sees human beings and natural things as interdependent and that definite ecological limits exist constraining economic development. If we assume that society and nature have a dialectical relationship which is shaped by the definite social relations specific to each mode of production, then as modes of production change so too does nature. For ecological approaches, the Marxist approach can pose a range of problems. Leaving aside, for the moment, the legacy of ecological damage within actual Marxist societies, ecologism rejects the idea that nature is determined by social relations and would challenge the idea that natural processes change with shifts in the mode of production.

Part of the attraction of Marxism lies in its language of transformation; both ecological and Marxist approaches assume that a solution to our problems can only be found through a fundamental change in human values and the way social life is organized. There are significant affinities in the way that they both pose an alternative social existence within which production would be simpler. The Marxist vision of communism assumes that production will be relatively simple in form and that the division of labour will be less complex than that which characterizes capitalist relations of production. This is a reflection of Marx's assumption that communism would abolish the exploitative commodity–wage relationship between employer and employee which gives capitalism its distinctive character and form. In particular, the continual drive for the expansion of productive capacity, which follows from the monopolistic tendency of capitalist production, will be absent. As Marx suggests:

> In communist society, where nobody has one exclusive sphere of activity but each can become accomplished in any branch he wishes, society regulates the general production and thus makes it possible for me to do one thing today and another tomorrow, to hunt in the morning, fish in the afternoon, rear cattle in the evening, criticise after

> dinner, just as I have a mind, without ever becoming hunter, fisherman, shepherd or critic . . .
>
> (Marx and Engels 1970: 54)

This points to a simpler way of life with human beings living in some degree of harmony with nature. It was this distinctive conception of an alternative social order that enabled Émile Durkheim to distinguish 'socialism', the expression of pain experienced by the lower classes at their condition, from 'communism', a backward step towards a less developed order. Nevertheless, in this statement, the underlying intent is to communicate the idea that labour power would be free of exploitation. This does not answer the questions raised by situations of over-fishing, over-hunting or over-grazing. Free labour does not in itself prevent ecological damage. Nor does this deal with large-scale productive processes which would be inherited from the capitalist mode of production. The transition to communism would simply change the ownership of property, not its capacity to inflict ecological damage or the treatment of natural things as valuable in so far as they can be used. The veteran ecological campaigner, Rudolf Bahro, has consistently warned that while reds and greens have a common foe, that of capitalism, ecological activists should not be blind to the continuing commitment of Marxists to industrialism and they should be wary of endorsing anti-capitalist arguments which are not grounded in ecologically sound assumptions (see Bahro 1986). In addition, it is important to recognize that socialist thought contains an element of scepticism about ecological concerns. Hans Enzensberger (1974) has expressed serious reservations about what he sees as the eclectic, apolitical, mystical and conservative tendencies of green activists. For these reasons, it is difficult to be both green and red at the same time. There are significant lessons to be learned from looking at the experience of Marxist societies which actually existed, if we are to explore the possibilities and limits of integrating Marxist and ecological thought.

The ecological disasters of the former Soviet bloc are now well known. The drive to produce socialism according to the principles of Marxism-Leninism, in relative isolation from the global capitalist market, ensured that the form of modernization process adopted was labour-intensive. In addition, little was done to limit waste production. The authoritarian nature of the political regime ensured that concern about ecological damage was silenced and political mobilization was suppressed in the pursuit of the national goal of the maximization of output. These societies, stretching from East Germany to North Korea, all attempted to compress the two-hundred-year process of industrialization into less than a human life-span. While the ecosystems which had experienced this in capitalist societies had two centuries to adjust to the human impacts involved, in state socialist societies the ecosystems were pushed to the limit by the level and intensity of natural resource extraction and waste disposal. This had dramatic effects on the people who worked in and lived near the productive processes involved, as well as the ecosystems they inhabited. From the standpoint of these Marxists, natural things were there for the taking. Within the strategy of 'socialism in one country', the primary goal was to overtake the Western capitalist societies in terms of material production. All other goals were subordinated to the maximization of output in agriculture, resource extraction and industrial production. The environmental effects of this kind of development strategy can be illustrated by the example of the Aral Sea. In this case, the water sources which previously fed into this vast inland lake were diverted for agricultural purposes. As a consequence, the sea was transformed into a barren salt lake and whole fishing fleets and harbour communities were left stranded in the desert as the sea shrank to almost a third of its previous size.

In other parts of the former Soviet bloc, whole areas were made uninhabitable, whether by nuclear radiation (for instance, around the Chernobyl nuclear plant) or by a range of airborne or water-borne pollutants. The *Environmental Action Programme for Central and Eastern Europe* (1993) identified a range of immediate problems in the former communist societies in eastern Europe including over-exposure to lead, acute and chronic respiratory conditions, high levels of infant mortality and lung cancer, as well as abnormal physiological development. In addition, there are significant problems in disposing of hazardous wastes. In these societies, we can see some of the most devastating consequences of unbridled industrialism. As a consequence, we should take the intuitive experiences and insights generated by people who experienced such exploitative processes very seriously. One of the most telling accounts of this type has been made by the playwright and political activist, Václav Havel:

As a boy, I lived for some time in the country and I clearly remember

> an experience from those days: I used to walk to school in a nearby village along a cart track through the fields and, on the way, see on the horizon a huge smokestack of some hurriedly built factory, in all likelihood in the service of war. It spewed dense smoke and scattered it across the sky. Each time I saw it, I had an intense sense of something profoundly wrong, of humans soiling the heavens. I have no idea whether there was something like a science of ecology in those days; if there was, I certainly knew nothing of it. That 'soiling of the heavens' nevertheless offended me spontaneously. It seemed to me that in so doing, humans are guilty of something, that they destroy something important, arbitrarily disrupting the natural order of things, and that such doings cannot go unpunished. . . . To me, personally, the smokestack soiling the heavens is not just a regrettable lapse of technology that failed to include 'the ecological factor' in its calculation, one which can be corrected easily with the appropriate filter. To me it is more the symbol of an age which seeks to transcend the boundaries of the natural world and its norms and to make it into a private concern, a matter of subjective preference and private feeling, of the illusions, prejudices and whims of a 'mere' individual. It is the symbol of an epoch which denies the binding importance of personal experience . . .
> (Havel 1988: 381–3)

Havel is commenting upon the 'Black Triangle' which exists across the national boundaries of the Czech Republic, Silesia (within Poland) and the former East Germany. People in this area experience shorter life expectancy and suffer from a much greater prevalence of respiratory illnesses and other diseases compared to people in neighbouring areas. Havel is raising the prospect of an approach to environmental ethics which draws upon personal experience and intuition rather than upon appeals to universal systems of rules or the sum total of human happiness. In the end, we should ask ourselves whether we are violating the natural order and think about ways of doing otherwise. In short, while Marxists today argue that attacking capitalism is the best immediate way of countering environmental pollution, it is not enough to change the ownership of production without transforming the way in which human beings produce things.

Political radicalism and the environment

In the previous section, we saw how the materialist foundations of Marxism led to a focus upon production in accounting for the relationship between society and nature. In particular, it was recognized that many of the key issues involved could be sensibly reinterpreted when we consider scarcity as historically and socially situated. This means that we can only make sense of a particular understanding of scarcity within a definite social and historical location. Indeed, for many Marxists, scarcity is a feature of a stable capitalist economy, that is, located within a definite set of productive relations and forces. For these reasons, Marxism offers a useful way for reconsidering the way we see nature, but not without significant qualifications. The privileged place of productive relations and forces in the Marxist approach, combined with its instrumental approach to nature, leaves open the possibility of the substantial exploitation of the environment. This ecological blind spot poses significant difficulties for integrating ecological and Marxist thought on the relationship between society and nature. Radical approaches, however, place a strong emphasis upon non-economic relations, particularly power relations, in diagnosing the problems confronting humanity. In this and the following section, we will explore two such approaches, anarchism and feminism. Both of these approaches offer radical ways of thinking about natural limitations on human activities in the context of definite situations and local practices.

Anarchist thought, much like ecological thought, can be found at many points on the political spectrum. Robert Nozick, for instance, who views nature as simply available for human use and sees obligations in terms of the respect for property rights, can be categorized as an individualistic anarchist and yet has much in common with neo-liberal approaches. Others, such as anarcho-communists, stress the importance of communal life although this approach, in common with all branches of anarchistic thought, contains a deep distrust of governing authorities. Despite such differences, anarchists are all committed to challenging the structure of a society which is founded upon rationalist principles. In particular, they challenge the idea that a rational answer can ever be taken to be the explanation of all human problems, ranging from how to produce things to making decisions democratically. In this sense, the anarchist approach acknowledges complexity and uncertainty in social relations. For anarchists, all attempts to construct authority are seen as attempts to control individuals and undermine their autonomy, whether this is political authority or authoritative knowledge.

The promise of anarchist thought stems from the idea that freedom from authority is a precondition for the spontaneous realization of the full capabilities and character of the individuals concerned. The anti-authority attitude has led some anarchists to propose small-scale and locally focused political projects, where all participants can be directly involved. Representative democracy is viewed as a political system based upon the apathy and resignation of citizens, and voting for political candidates is seen as an abdication of responsibility for managing one's own affairs. In order to overcome the hierarchical power structures which characterize advanced industrial societies, anarchists propose direct democracy. So, in the place of government, anarchists propose self-government, with all members of a community participating in the decision-making processes which affect the collective existence of the community concerned. These ideas have had an enormous impact upon the political structure of ecological groups, organizations and movements.

Green parties have often experimented with a variety of anti-elitist organizational structures such as rotating leadership patterns, conference discussions (such as table-talk) and decentralized decision-making processes. However, within the conventional party system, which is hierarchical, elitist and competitive, where quick responses and effective leadership are seen as crucial, green parties which adopt anarchist-oriented political structures are at a disadvantage. As a response, ecological thought stresses the need for a transformation of the political system itself in order to prevent political parties competing for support with promises of higher levels of economic growth, with all the attendant impacts upon the environment that continual improvements in the material standard of living tend to involve. Anarchists, like all currents of radical politics, identify power relations as the problem; politics involves relations of oppression and exploitation throughout all aspects of human existence. By diagnosing the problems of society as political ones rather than solely economic ones, as in the case of Marxism, anarchists suggest that they can only be solved through a transformation of the power relations in the state, economy and culture.

The language of transformation adopted by anarchists has led many to see these approaches as supportive of violent change. Some anarchists have advocated political violence, but no more so than any other ideological movement. It should also be noted that anarchism is grounded upon a wealth of pacifist literature, such as the writings of Tolstoy and Gandhi. These writings emphasize non-violent direct action strategies as a means of securing change when conventional forms of political activity and persuasion have proved to be ineffective. Consequently, given the resistance to ecological concerns by governments and business, many environmental organizations have drawn upon anarchist principles to push an issue up the agenda or even to prevent a particular form of pollution or resource extraction taking place. In the remainder of this section, we will concentrate on two examples where the ideas of anarchism have come into contact with ecological thought: social ecology and eco-communalism.

The most prominent social ecologist, Murray Bookchin, developed his position by working through some of the difficulties of Marxist thinking when understanding nature. Bookchin has been concerned to develop an approach which contains a more 'libertarian' account of social organization than that which has often emerged from Marxist thinking. In particular, he has sought to challenge the idea of 'social hierarchy' which characterizes both capitalist and socialist social orders. For Bookchin, the domination of nature is a product of the domination of humans by other humans (initially in terms of age and gender but later in terms of race, caste and class); these relations of dominance have become the institutional basis of human societies. In its place, Bookchin wishes to establish relations of interdependence between living and non-living natural things, but which do not involve hierarchy, exploitation or domination. He contends that human beings have lost contact with the natural processes which act as the conditions of their existence. Bookchin avoids the tendency to attribute social qualities to the complex and uncertain relations of ecosystems but suggests that human beings have a conscious and vital role to play within the evolutionary processes at work in nature. Human beings, he suggests, could replace the socially produced idea of 'hierarchy' with the recognition of 'variation' and the 'complementary linkages' which predominate in ecosystems.

Bookchin is concerned not only to counter instrumental conceptions of natural things but also to highlight the mistaken tendencies of deep ecology to view human beings as inconsequential in the long-term development of natural processes and relations, as 'parasites' on the surface of the earth. Instead, he argues, human beings have a vital role to play as 'ecological stewards' in the evolutionary process, consciously engaged in the negotiated relationship between society and nature. Of course, it is hard to imagine such stewardship without the use of the same processes of human reason which have done so much damage in the first place. This claim presents a problem for, while Bookchin does acknowledge complexity and uncertainty in evolution, human decisions are made on the basis of simplistic assumptions, with limited knowledge and understanding of the processes involved and, in evolutionary terms, very short-term considerations. This means that human decisions will usually have a range of unintended consequences which will make ecological stewardship an unpredictable enterprise. We have only to look at the history of science – for example, the development of nuclear power – to demonstrate some of the terrible consequences of having too much confidence in human reason. The idea of 'Atoms for Peace' was so persuasive because it appeared to offer a relatively clean way of generating unlimited power. Similar unintended consequences will emerge through genetic engineering and biotechnological interventions. The social ecology approach conceals a rationalist's confidence in what can be done through human knowledge. Bookchin himself states the difficulty involved in understanding nature because

> evolution is open and indeterminate. There is no goal in it, or purpose, and yet there is a recognisable pattern of development. The details of this pattern are unpredictable because of the autonomy living systems possess in their evolution as in other aspects of their organisation.
> (Bookchin 1980: 195)

Thus, social ecology presents us with a useful way of identifying the dilemmas involved instead of helping us resolve them. In the second example of anarchist thought on the environment we turn to eco-communalism, with its more explicitly ecocentric orientation. This approach offers a more pro-active response to the issues identified by Bookchin, by attempting to find a way of creating localized, small-scale, autonomous, cooperative communities while, at the same time, maintaining respect for non-human things. Eco-communalist approaches possess a greater humility than does Bookchin's account of ecological stewardship, for they see the human species as part of the web of life rather than the masters of it. The attractiveness of this strategy can be seen in its wide appeal, ranging from Edward Goldsmith's classic 'Blueprint for Survival' (1972) to Rudolf Bahro's spiritual challenge to ecological degradation in industrial societies (Bahro 1986), from Fritz Schumacher's claim that *Small is Beautiful* (1973) to Kirkpatrick Sale's account of bioregional communities (Sale, 1985). These diverse writers have one thing in common, a distrust of the human capacity to know and understand fully what our species is doing to nature. Contemporary societies, argues Schumacher, possess considerable 'know-how' but they have very little in the way of 'know-what' – they lack moral guidelines on what to do about what they know! Knowledge carries duties and obligations, it can never be value-free.

Bioregionalists place a strong emphasis upon self-sufficiency, cooperation and diversity (both biological and social). In addition, they stress the importance of developing a *politics of obligation*, to foster a sense of responsibility to the (social) community, humankind and the biotic community. The bioregionalist movement, in this sense, has many affinities with the kind of conservatism presented by John Gray, but also draws upon the support of socialists, feminists and anarchists. The movement has been criticized for its romanticism and utopianism, an accusation made against all anarchist movements. However, we should also bear in mind that the use of these labels in such a derogatory way is closely tied to the belief held by critics that the march of progress can never be challenged. The most common objection pertains to the idea of returning to a simpler life, a pre-industrial past. Certainly, eco-communalist solutions would involve a fairly substantial transformation, but the strength of these approaches rests on their critique of unnecessary complexity in social organization. For instance, they ask whether it is necessary to transport fruit and vegetables from one part of the globe to another, distorting the agricultural practices of producer communities who come to rely on cash crops, merely to satisfy the desires of the wealthier sections of the human species. This leaves the incomes of producer communities vulnerable to market and climatic changes and, in addition, undermines the local diversity of food supplies in the consuming community. The accusations of romanticism are a little unfair, although eco-communalist activists sometimes make a virtue out of the romantic interpretation of natural things. In effect, however, these approaches simply state how it is possible to construct sustainable forms of social organization as an alternative to the existing exploitative uses of natural things. The principles of bioregionalism, in particular, do draw something from the practices and experiences of earlier societies, but they also draw from past mistakes. Simpler societies have also managed to damage their own ecosystems to the point where the societies involved have collapsed.

Looking at different forms of social organization enables us to think about what has previously been unthinkable, to question the idea that societies should be based upon permanent growth and human mastery over nature. As a response, bioregionalism attempts to find ways of developing small human communities with naturally formed bioregions, discrete ecological areas composed of an interrelated set of life forms and physical characteristics. It is also assumed that the scale of any human community depends on the carrying capacity of the respective bioregions, which are themselves quite varied. Urban centres would not be completely isolated but would be connected through networks, enabling centres to cooperate on problems which cannot be resolved by the members of a local community on their own. In this way, social organization would be collaborative rather than hierarchical.

For Martin W. Lewis, in *Green Delusions* (1992), the aspiration to reconstruct social relations in such a way as to remove hierarchical organizations makes the whole bioregional approach impractical and misunderstands social organization. For a start, he argues that it is virtually impossible to identify and demarcate ecologically distinct regions in practical terms, because species overlap and interact in complex changing ways. Lewis is right to recognize that small can be ugly as well as beautiful (that small communities offer no ecological guarantees). However, by focusing upon the size of human communities, he misses the point that Schumacher makes, that the form of human activity should be ecologically appropriate to the situation in question. This is why there are no simple, all-purpose answers to ecological problems. Moreover, Lewis rests his case upon a stark contrast between fantastic ecotopias and the cold remorseless logic of capital accumulation orchestrated by hard-headed bureaucratic corporate capitalism. The alternative, he suggests, involves the steady humanization of existing political, economic and cultural institutions and the development of 'realistic plans' and 'concrete strategies for avoiding ecological collapse and reconstructing an ecologically sustainable economic order' (Lewis 1992: 250). By 'realism', he means a moderate liberal alliance in order to find a balance between social progress and environmental protection. However, Lewis focuses solely upon ideal blueprint solutions rather than the reasons for developing the eco-communalist approaches in the first place. This critique of ecological thought rests firmly upon unacknowledged anthropocentric assumptions – human institutions need ecologizing, not humanizing!

Clearly, bioregional advocates presume that human beings have the level of knowledge and the depth of understanding of the green environment to plan a bioregional solution. However, human knowledge is incomplete and patchy and is likely to remain so in the face of a constantly changing object of analysis. If we take on board this note of caution then we can use the bioregional approach as a way of thinking strategically and flexibly about what forms of living are appropriate in the variety of environmental situations inhabited by human beings. No single mode of social organization is likely to provide a unique way of delivering the goals of ecological thought. No single blueprint will do, what is needed is a 'greenprint', a strategic orientation which acknowledges the complexity and uncertainty of the changing relationships between society and nature. In the next section, on eco-feminism, we will explore an approach which contains a deeper scepticism about claims to know, an approach which draws a close connection between the domination of nature and the domination of women.

Feminist thinking and ecology

In this section, we will examine the ways in which feminism has contributed to ecological thought and how this has, in turn, led many feminists to question their own assumptions. The reason why these two developments are connected stems from the nature of discussions within feminism about the relationship between gender, nature, culture and science. For the sake of brevity, and in recognition of the breadth of feminist opinion, we must focus upon radical feminism and its portrayal of the relations of power as patriarchal. Liberal, socialist and Marxist variants of feminism will be viewed as covered by the previous sections of this chapter. The (radical) feminist consideration of nature is shaped, at least in part, by the way in which femininity has been regarded as closer to nature, and masculinity as closer to culture, within Western societies. In modern societies, where progress is identified as a consequence of the human mastery over natural forces for human good, scientific knowledge plays a crucial role in transforming natural things into products for human use. It is not surprising, then, that the dialogue between ecological and feminist thought has focused upon the interrelations between the exploitation of nature and the exploitation of women. All human beings have benefited from the exploitation of natural things although in varying ways, with women historically receiving less than their fair share. This raises questions about whether the feminist approach, which has been committed to the emancipation of women, as part of humanity, is actually compatible with ecologism, which asks all human beings to limit their material aspirations and carefully think through the implications of their activities in ecological terms.

The connection between the domination of nature and the domination of women is particularly stressed in the writings of Carolyn Merchant. In *The Death of Nature* (1980), Merchant charts the ways in which scientific thinking emerged during the early modern period, as part of the processes through which the relations of production and reproduction became the passive and controlled objects of a male-dominated social order. Science, as the embodiment of a male order, would ensure the control of the 'disorderly woman' and the 'chaotic state of nature'. From this viewpoint, science is seen as an extension of the witch-hunts in the sixteenth and seventeenth centuries. Merchant suggests that an older order of nature – of 'uncivilized wilderness', of the 'bestiality' of uncolonized peoples, of the 'sexual lust of the female' and of base 'animal passions' in all human beings – had died and was replaced by a new order in which nature, women and indigenous peoples of the newly discovered parts of the globe were all subordinated.

> A new experimental method designed to constrain nature and probe her secrets would improve and 'civilize' society. The macrocosm

> would become a machine consistent with new managerial modes of order and power.
>
> (Merchant 1980: 148)

Maria Mies and Vandana Shiva have also identified strong patriarchal assumptions in the foundations of science, notably the distinction between mind and body which relegated women's concerns as closer to nature than to culture and science. The metaphors used by Bacon served to reinforce the gendered nature of science throughout the modern period. For Bacon, nature should be controlled, subordinated and 'forced by torture to yield her secrets, like a bad woman who keeps her treasures avariciously to herself and withholds them from her . . . sons' (Mies and Shiva 1993: 44). The emergence of science is also seen as deeply implicated in the naturalization of femininity in this period, whereby masculinity becomes associated with culture and learning while femininity becomes associated with nature. Feminist interpretations of these processes have suggested that the institutional exclusion of women from culture, art, literature and the natural sciences can also be related to the emerging modern distinction between the public domain, where power and autonomy are defined, and the private sphere, regarded as the sphere of consumption, leisure and personal relations. Where femininity and nature did exist within scientific discourse, it was almost invariably in the form of the object of analysis.

Within the writings of ecofeminists such as Merchant, Mies and Shiva, we have seen the emergence of a new mode of enquiry, which argues that any project to emancipate women should also embrace the means of liberating nature from oppression. This theme is taken up and developed by Andrée Collard and Joyce Contrucci in *The Rape of the Wild* (1988), where they assert that the experience of abuse and mistreatment, combined with the experience of motherhood, means that women are uniquely placed to understand ecological problems and issues. In addition to women having a more profound sense of ecological damage, they suggest, women are also best placed to find and implement a remedy for such abuses. In particular, they point to a different attitude towards nature, even among those who wish to defend the environment. Collard examines *The Wooing of Earth* (1980) by René Dubos to demonstrate the difficulties in identifying an appropriate environmental ethic free from masculine forms of power and control. In this case, she suggests, the idea of 'wooing' contains connotations of a heroic quest which involves a masculine agent actively seeking to subdue and conquer the passive female receptacle.

The language of heroes and seduction is demonstrated through the consideration of landscape formation by Dubos; nature is only fully realized through human intervention. The landscape takes form and awakes from slumber through the kiss of the human prince or at least the technical skills and money-making talents of planners, landscape designers and farmers. For Dubos, nature does not know best and it should not be left to its own devices. In such an approach, the sculpted gardens of Capability Brown represent the epitome of nature's true promise. However, for Collard:

> To 'love' the earth as potential is equivalent to loving women as potential that remains unexpressed until properly manipulated by man's labour and imagination. 'Love' without reciprocity is exploitation.
> (Collard and Contrucci 1988: 145)

In the place of such attitudes, Collard emphasizes the importance of the nurturing values associated with motherhood as a way of reconstructing a caring but respectful attitude towards nature. With women as the vanguard of the ecofeminist movement, this involves

> a caring that extends far beyond the vulgar concern that as we lose 'the environment' we imperil human survival. They not only love nature, beauty, and life but are bold enough to own their anger at their violation and have a heart to empathise with pain. In short, they are dedicated to the well-being of life for the sake of life.
> (Collard and Contrucci 1988: 142)

At the heart of this approach is a respect for life absent from anthropocentric approaches to natural things. The label 'ecofeminism' was introduced by Ynestra King and gained credence through the 1980 Conference on 'Women and Life on Earth', established to counter the life-threatening activities of nuclear weapons and nuclear power. Judith Plant argues that the values of women are centred upon the creation and maintenance of life and, as such, the experiences of child-rearing can provide a model of good ecological practice and healing the wounds caused by present exploitative practices (see Plant 1989). The ecofeminist approach, therefore, takes the feminine traits which are devalued within Western patriarchal cultures and revalues them as a basis for defining strategies for preventing ecological damage and for developing sustainable social orders. Mies and Shiva cite the experience of women and children in developing societies as a useful illustration of the ways in which their understandings of poverty and 'environmental degradation' can point the way to change. In particular, the resistance movements which women have organized against logging, pollution and specific disasters, such as the toxic leak at Bhopal in India, have provided a model for future activism with the emphasis upon the household.

The problem with this approach stems from its over-dependence upon the idea of female traits in defining gender-specific behaviour. In particular, ecofeminism fails to account for the origin of 'feminine values' within a patriarchal social order. The idea of nature, according to Valerie Plumwood, is a conservative device for keeping women in a subordinate position. Notions of 'proper' feminine values tend to emphasize passivity, timidity, obedience and modesty rather than independent thought, rationality and self-interest. The adoption of passive values, in conjunction with a contrast with assertive masculine values, has been described by a number of feminists as the main reason for women becoming the 'architects of their own oppression' (see Stacey and Price 1981). For Plumwood, the best starting point would be a 'degendered' one, which degraded neither nature nor femininity (see Plumwood 1990). The lessons drawn from the over-dependence of women upon scientific and technological solutions to their problems are amply illustrated by Mies and Shiva (1993). Women in developing societies around the world found that they had been used as 'guinea-pigs' by Western pharmaceutical companies trying out contraceptive devices prior to sale in the West. Rather than being a means to liberation, contraceptive technology had serious health consequences for many of the women involved.

In *Earth Follies* (1993), Joni Seager argues that the environmentalist and green activist movements are themselves shaped by androcentric and anthropocentric concerns. Seager concentrates her fire upon the 'ecology establishment' as much as on the corporate business sector, governments and the military. In particular, Seager suggests that the professionalization of environmental organizations since the 1960s and their transformation into lobbying machines has led to a proliferation of 'eco-bureaucracies' in the political systems of Western societies. The organizations she has in mind are the Sierra Club and Friends of the Earth, which have worked within existing political arrangements and legal systems to further the cause of the environment. It is these organizations, rather than grass-roots activists, she argues, which shape the agenda on environmental policy-making. For this reason, feminist concerns have been largely ignored in the emergence of environmental politics. She concludes that what we have witnessed in the last two decades is, at most, the 'greening of men's politics'. For Seager, the

> sudden inflation in political green currency has come at a high cost to the Greens themselves. While the Greens have introduced green values into conventional political arenas, the relationship has cut both ways. Mainstream politics has transformed the Green agenda, even the internal structure of Green parties. Many of the established Green parties have become fractured by internal divisions and fragmented by hot disputes over policies and strategies. Green values have not always fared well in translation. The Green commitment to feminist values seems to have especially suffered in the course of the Green transformation into a mainstream political force.
>
> (Seager 1993: 170)

For Seager, the commitment to an anti-elitist politics and to the recognition of women's issues in political debates, which ecofeminists pioneered in the early green parties, has been sacrificed, either wholly or in part, as part of the process of presenting acceptable policies to the electorate. In particular, she highlights evidence that in Western societies men's and women's attitudes to environmental problems differ markedly. The male valuation of natural things was considerably more oriented towards conserving wildlife for self-serving purposes such as hunting, and the male perspective on the maintenance of natural habitats was in terms of yields and harvesting. The female perspective, they argue, conserve for different reasons than men, they conserve to maintain a healthier and less polluted environment. Within the eco-establishment, Seager argues, it is male concerns which dominate in the management and conservation of natural habitats. Seager also raises significant problems about the character and activities of eco-activists, in organizations such as Earth First. In particular, she criticizes its macho-heroic direct action politics and its tendency to respond to critics in mysogynistic and homophobic terms:

> Earth Firsters are not just men; they are 'men's men'. Dave Foreman, one of the founders of the American Earth First! movement,

> represented the tone and the tenor of the group when he said that, 'I see Earth First! as a warrior society'. The leaders of Earth First revelled in an image of themselves as beer-swilling, ass-kicking, 'dumb cowboy rednecks' coming to the rescue of a helpless female – in this case, Mother Earth.
>
> (Seager 1993: 227)

Ecofeminist approaches highlight some of the dangers of ecological activism but also demonstrate the way in which all forms of knowledge are situated within a specific historical and cultural location. Ecological thought has emerged within the context of the highly mechanized androcentric cultures of Western industrial societies. With this mind, it is not surprising that eco-activists draw upon their own cultural values to make sense of the ways in which they are challenging anthropocentric values. The questions raised by ecofeminists prompt us to reconsider the relationship between anthropocentrism and androcentrism, but any suggestion that they are synonymous should be viewed with considerable scepticism. Just as it is possible to envisage an ecocentric human society with strong patriarchal values, so is it also possible to imagine a society based upon androgyny with extensive ecological damage and exploitation.

Ecological thought and emancipation

This chapter began to explore the challenges posed by ecological thought for the values and assumptions of the traditional political homes of ecological activists, that is, social and political movements on the left. Along the way, certain features of these movements were identified as having some potential for incorporation within ecological thought, or at least they demonstrated some compatibility with ecocentric values. In particular, political projects for human emancipation, either from oppressive political systems or from economic exploitation, place an important emphasis upon the relationship between the idea of justice and the need to avoid environmental damage. However, this is overshadowed by the instrumental view of nature within emancipatory projects and the tendency to adopt a human-centred conception of a just social order. The experience of 'actually collapsing socialisms' also highlights the potential for left ideologies to create more ecological damage than capitalist social orders. However, while there are significant tensions between ecological and socialist thought, socialism provides one of the most powerful reasons for taking the environment seriously, that is, the improvement of the health and welfare of the human species. However, the adoption of such values can offer only a partial remedy unless the way in which things are produced is changed as well.

The various forms of radical thought considered in this chapter shift the emphasis from production to questions of power. The relationship between ecological thought and anarchist and feminist variants of radicalism, especially their political strategies, is a particularly important one. Anarchists have consistently criticized concentrations of power and the dangers of 'grand visions of transformation' associated with Marxism. In practice, anarchists have had only short-lived and limited success in changing the way social orders are constructed. However, their experimentation with localized and small-scale community building offers a fertile ground for identifying alternative forms of social organization which do not have the same impact on ecosystems as the practices of advanced industrial economies. The focus upon self-sufficiency and responsibility to the local ecosystem provides the basis for thinking about what it must be like to construct a society which tries to respect nature rather than seeking human mastery. Ecofeminist thinking also seeks to break with the idea of mastery but emphasizes the ways in which this is closely connected to the mastery of men over women within human societies.

There is, of course, no essential link between projects which encourage respect for nature and wanting people to be free of unwanted forms of authority and control. Similarly, it is possible to envisage situations where the interests of women come into conflict with living in harmony with the ecosystems inhabited by human beings. However, in both ecoanarchist and ecofeminist approaches we have seen the emergence of potential strategies for change and models of social life which are less damaging than many existing societies and communities. Perhaps most importantly, both approaches raise fundamental questions about the role of rational human knowledge in the subjugation of natural forces. Ecofeminism goes further in identifying the androcentric basis of 'objective knowledge' in order to show how male-centred prejudices masquerade as scientific truth. Clearly, the relationship between instrumental conceptions of nature and the role of science in controlling natural things is a very close one. In the final chapter, we will question the role of scientific knowledge in understanding environmental hazards.

6
The Prospects for Ecological Citizenship

Three themes have been at the centre of discussion throughout the previous chapters: first, the complicated problems involved in defining obligations and their limits; second, the connections between existing social and political theory and ecological thought; and third, the need to rethink conventional ethical assumptions by replacing anthropocentric with ecocentric values, and so creating new possibilities for changing the relationship between society and nature. At the centre of this intellectual project is the firm conviction that conventional conceptions of justice and citizenship do not provide the human species with an adequate set of tools for resolving the difficulties created by ecological damage today. Earlier, it was argued that this sort of transformation did not require a 'blueprint', an ideal ecotopia worked out to the last detail, but a 'greenprint'. This 'greenprint' should not only acknowledge the complexity, uncertainty and interconnectedness of the relations between society and nature, but also provide a set of working principles which can be used for developing flexible strategies for change.

Contemporary interventions on the environment

In this final chapter, it is useful to identify the alternative ways of theorizing these issues. Three attempts to provide such an account stand out in recent social theory: the social construction approach;

the realist approach; and the theory of the risk society. We will briefly consider the first two and then turn in more detail to the risk society approach, which addresses the concerns of complexity, uncertainty and interconnectedness much more directly.

The social construction approach asserts that all accounts of nature are a social product and that they reveal more about the cultures which produce them than about natural processes themselves. In this way, Keith Tester suggests, the increase in concern for animal welfare and animal rights is a reflection of changing cultural values and the way in which we view ourselves. In this way, natural objects and animals become 'blank paper which can be inscribed with any message' (Tester 1991: 46). Similarly, Steven Yearley argues that environmental problems are constructed through the interpretation and activities of groups of social actors, such as the mass media and scientific communities, rather than existing in any objective sense (see Yearley 1991). In this way, environmental problems are a product of the human imagination rather than real problems. From the point of view of ecologism, the treatment of human impacts upon the green environment as no more than a 'social construct' operates as a euphemism for neglect and indifference to environmental concerns.

The realist approach has been developed in the study of the environment by Peter Dickens in *Society and Nature* (1992). Realism also recognizes that we can only grasp nature through language and culture but treat the structures of natural objects as real. In this approach, structures involve causal powers (they enable human beings to do things) as well as limitations (acknowledged and unacknowledged constraints) upon human action. For instance, natural objects have the capacity to act upon human life, just as a turbulent weather system still involves real forces at work. The physical damage of this turbulence remains unaltered whether we interpret it as a storm or a hurricane. In the same way, regardless of the social constructions about natural habitats, the capacity of a local ecosystem to cope with large amounts of pollution poses a real limit upon human activities. At some point, the concentration of pollutants will cause the ecosystem to collapse, just as pollution can have real effects upon the life chances of individuals. In this sense, environmental problems are real problems, even though we may represent them in various ways.

Certainly, realism offers a perspective which can accommodate the complex interrelationship between society and nature. In addition, it draws our attention to the way in which forms of social organization are made by human beings and can therefore be changed by them. This approach is often drawn upon to provide a theory of knowledge for social and political theories with social transformation in mind, such as Marxism. Nevertheless, the normative thrust of realism is one based upon 'human' emancipation, that scientific knowledge is the means through which human beings can reject one set of exploitative structures in favour of 'wanted determinations'. The anthropocentricity of realism and its socialist leanings remain a major problem for ecological thought which, instead, seeks to find new ways of thinking through the human relationship with the green environment based upon ecocentric assumptions.

In the third approach, developed by the social theorists Anthony Giddens and Ulrich Beck, we can find an explicit recognition of the limitations of human knowledge. In this approach, it is argued that 'objective' scientific accounts of natural processes no longer offer an effective explanation of the human impact on the natural world. For Giddens, we have entered a new phase of social development, characterized by uncertainty and anxiety, in which science can offer little reassurance (see Giddens 1990; Beck *et al.* 1994). All human choices involve an element of risk, for the consequences of our actions can no longer be predicted with any degree of certainty, whether this involves the consumption of beef or immunization of children. In some ways, people have experienced a reduction of risk over the last century, as exemplified by the progress made in combating disease. Nevertheless, the nature of risk, and specifically of environmental hazards, has now changed to such an extent that the incidence, effects and interrelationships between them cannot be effectively predicted and our responses planned out in advance. The next section focuses exclusively on this approach, on the consequences of living within a 'risk society' (Beck 1992; 1995).

The risk society and environmental degradation

For Ulrich Beck, environmental hazards can never be eliminated through the use of technological knowledge, although they can be anticipated. He claims that we now live in a 'risk society' and yet we draw answers to these problems from the logic of the nineteenth century. While the hazards of a technologically driven society in the late twentieth century 'penetrate every region and level of society', human beings remain wedded to the responses to environmental degradation which were more appropriate in the nineteenth century. In industrial societies, he suggests, risks were calculable and fault or blame could be clearly identified. The welfare system and associated forms of private insurance are all manifestations of the confident logic of the 'safety state', whereby clear rules of conduct existed for attributing causal responsibility and awarding compensation. However, in the 'risk society' which we presently inhabit, no such guarantees exist. The scale and scope of human impacts upon the environment produce a range of complex and unanticipated consequences which cannot be contained effectively within the earlier guarantees and safety mechanisms. In addition, whereas in industrial societies the lower classes were also likely to experience the worst effects of industrial pollution, in the 'risk society' all social groups are susceptible to the effects of pollution.

> As the floodgates of poison open (through the absence of maximum pollution levels, inapplicable principles of causal attribution and juridical fictions), an explosive political situation emerges. In the omnipresence of harmful substances, a spark of information ignited by the mass media can destroy whole markets and industries. The victims cannot be specified or determined in advance. Where despoliation is unattributable, the economy, the public and the media begin to play Russian roulette under cover of the category of 'environmental' hazards deriving from a different age.
>
> (Beck 1995: 10)

When the stakes are so high, Beck argues, it is necessary to reflect critically upon the way in which scientific interpretations of environmental hazards operate in relation to the political systems in which environmental problems are defined, understood and acted upon. For Beck, we must start by recognizing the danger of the 'organized irresponsibility' which is built into the institutional forms of modern industrial societies. 'Organized irresponsibility' refers to the subtle ways in which elite groups fail to acknowledge the seriousness of the problems they confront as well as the ways in which our knowledge and understanding of environmental issues are so constructed that 'danger becomes normality'. The idea of 'organized irresponsibility' appears to be drawn from the classic attack on the military-industrial complex in the closing passages of

The Power Elite (1956) by C. Wright Mills. In this case, it is applied to the ways in which political, economic and cultural agenda-blenders blind themselves and everyone else to the perils of environmental degradation. This process of normalization, whereby the enormous risks now produced by human activities are translated into acceptable costs, Beck argues, conceals the potential explosiveness of environmental hazards.

The way in which environmental risks are presently calculated depends upon a vocabulary which reflects the assumptions of the interests of polluting industries rather than of those affected. The onus of proof of damage remains with the victim, rather than with the polluter. However, in the case of the effect of nuclear waste or toxic chemicals, proof is particularly difficult to establish. For instance, a wide range of potential carcinogens exist and it is particularly difficult to single out nuclear power as a causal factor in, for instance, leukaemia, even when leaks of radioactive material can be established. So, in such cases, compensation is rarely awarded. Beck suggests that this is further complicated because it is no longer feasible to distinguish between social life and natural processes, for these exist inside each other. For Beck, scientific practice and the comforting reassurances of experts are part of the problem, rather than offering a perfect solution. When we assess the problems facing the human species in the twenty-first century, Beck suggests that we should be aware that the very means of identifying environmental problems, scientific knowledge, has itself contributed to those problems. So where do we go from here?

Beck begins to sketch the possible futures involved. We can, of course, continue to apply solutions appropriate to an industrial society within a risk society, with all the potential dangers involved in maintaining present human activities. Ecological thought clearly rules this out. Two further responses remain. The first is a strong state response whereby the existing political institutions consolidate their power and exert a greater control over potential hazards. This 'authoritarian technocracy' would attempt to shore up the social institutions which were the cause of the problem while exerting greater controls over the activities involved. This is the 'health and safety state' advocated by social democrats. In this approach, the central principle of the Enlightenment, the rational pursuit of knowledge, is used to tame industrialism. For Beck, with each batch of regulations and legislative measures, we would witness an extension of state power and control as well as its centralization in the hands of an elite which controlled knowledge and expertise. The definition of what was safe and what was a hazard would remain in the hands of 'those who know best'. From the standpoint of ecological thought, the road to ecological degradation is paved with the intentions of technocrats who thought they knew best. Past experience would suggest that this route is unlikely to be a fruitful one.

The other response Beck proposes is 'ecological democracy', an approach which would involve a substantial reorientation of social existence and the rules of conduct which organize it. Like most projects for social change, this is defined through its negation of existing arrangements and the principles which underpin them: the emergence of technological change only from a thorough discussion of the possible consequences (rather than its imposition from above); a transformation of the basis of proof in the legal rules which refer to environmental risk assessment; and the presumption that potential polluters would have to prove the safety of productive processes (rather than the afflicted proving they have been adversely affected). These are all positive steps in purely anthropocentric terms but, in terms of ecological thought, there are significant problems in making decisions purely in terms of whether human beings are affected adversely. Certainly, the restriction of human activities envisaged by Beck would be fairly dramatic and much of the potential damage would be avoided. However, risk avoidance would not necessarily promote respect for the environment, just help the human species to protect its own hide.

Towards ecological citizenship

At this point it is useful to bring together the arguments developed in the previous chapters and use them to reconsider the position of humanity in relation to nature. In particular, this involves acknowledging complexity, uncertainty and the interconnectedness of society and nature. In short, it should be recognized that ecological thought has many affinities with risk society approaches. The approach developed by Beck, however, could be significantly transformed through the insertion of ecocentric premises. It is this combination of ideas which could offer a way of thinking through the assumptions and implications of ecological citizenship.

First, in order to explore the problem of defining a moral

community and the difficulties of defining moral boundaries, we considered the difficulties of future jeopardy and human relations with non-human animals. When we consider our obligations to future generations, especially in the light of the range of 'time bombs with long fuses' and the variety of ways in which present generations are discriminating against future generations, we can see how arbitrary the moral boundary between present and future generations of human beings really is. One responsible way we can avoid the risks involved (as we explored in Chapter 2) is to reconsider present actions with this in mind – present generations should not act in ways which jeopardize the existence of future generations and their ability to live in dignity, and, if we do act in ways which contain the possibility of adverse future consequences, we should minimize such risks. Thus, if we are to address the needs of future strangers, we should act as if the consequences of our actions could harm our own children. While this limits moral consideration to human beings there is no reason, other than prejudice, why this should not be extended to non-human animals and other natural things.

By extending the moral community we are attributing intrinsic value to creatures and other natural things, as ends in themselves rather than the means to some set of human ends. This displaces the human species from its dominant position within the ecosystem. In ethical terms, any set of moral rules should consider these duties towards non-human animals, the land, forests and woodland, the oceans, mountains and the biosphere. If such an ethical system were to be adopted, then moral governance would shift from the application of principles to the application of moral frameworks, that is, the network of mutually supportive principles, theories, and attitudes toward consequences (see Stone 1987). In this way, by focusing upon the ethical context of each situation, we can identify the appropriate moral guidance for particular historical and cultural locations. Nevertheless, we still need to bear in mind the problem that the green environment is only intelligible through the lenses of the human imagination, even if we tend to assume that nature and 'the natural' are definite things beyond humanity. To prepare the way for the emergence of a plurality of moral frameworks, we also need to address the political context through which ethical standpoints are translated into effective actions. Ethical systems do not exist in a vacuum, but tend to be meaningful within definite social orders.

It is at this point that we should consider the role of citizenship in helping us towards a better understanding of the issues raised. Citizenship refers to the framework of complex interlocking relations which exist between obligations and entitlements in any legal and moral system. In the modern period we have so far witnessed three phases of citizenship: civil citizenship, political citizenship and social citizenship. The establishment of *civil citizenship* established property ownership rights and a corresponding set of obligations to respect the possessions of other property owners. Property ownership also acted as the basis of political rights, with access to decision-making institutions only permitted to those with a personal stake in society (for it was accepted that property ownership generated a sense of responsibility to the maintenance of social order). In the second phase, *political citizenship* involved an extension of voting rights to all members of society on the grounds that, as members of the political, legal and moral community, they should have some say in the decision-making processes which affected their lives. The emergence of free speech, free association, freedom of mobility and voting rights carried with it a series of obligations to avoid libel, slander and sedition and to prevent public disorder. The continuation of membership of this community thus depends upon following the rules of the political game and abiding by the procedures for reform. Finally, with *social citizenship*, the emergence of welfare rights carries with it certain obligations to contribute to the funds established for the provision of the needs of strangers. Within the terms of social citizenship, experiences such as unemployment, sickness, destitution, squalor and so on, which had been previously regarded as personal difficulties, became subject to state intervention on behalf of the collective order.

In each of these forms of citizenship the connections between entitlements and obligations are grounded in the recognition that we should treat others in ways in which we would like to be treated. In short, each phase of citizenship is connected to a particular idea of justice. In addition, all of these relations of entitlement and obligation are founded upon the liberal distinction between private and public spheres – a space should exist where political authority has a limited role. In each of these forms of citizenship, the distinction between what is private and what is public moves but the distinction itself remains unquestioned. *Ecological citizenship*, however, questions the efficacy of this distinction, for the relations of entitlement and obligation break through the species barrier and beyond. In ecological thought, human beings have obligations to animals, trees, mountains, oceans, and other members of the biotic community. This means that human beings have to exercise extreme caution before embarking upon any project which is likely to have the possibility of adverse effects upon the ecosystems concerned. The limits that this places upon human action are severe and no existing political vocabulary has managed to capture this transformation in the relationship between society and nature.

Ecological citizenship will lead the human species into a fundamental reassessment of its capacities for acting upon the environment. The complexity, uncertainty and increased interconnectedness of all living things and their life support systems, make a reassessment of human obligations even more imperative. Many basic personal choices which were previously considered inviolable will be subject to challenge. This involves more than a further shift in the public–private boundary, for it means the demise of the distinction itself. In such a situation, the institutional embodiments of the private and public spheres, that is, civil society and the state, will be in doubt. For Beck, as we have seen, we face two choices: 'authoritarian technocracy', the absorption of civil society by the state; or 'ecological democracy', the absorption of the state by civil society. The purpose of this text is to raise the prospect of a further fundamental shift in the human politico-ethical life world. In Beck's account of 'ecological democracy', the liberal distinction between the public and the private becomes questionable but the moral community remains human-centred. While human beings become more sensitive to the unanticipated consequences of their actions, the basis of the social order remains fixed upon human needs and desires. However, the only effective way to change the way in which humans regard natural things is to change their relationship with the environment. Ecological citizenship not only challenges the distinction between the public and private spheres, but also transforms the nature of the moral community itself, by displacing the human species from the central ethical position it has always held. In short, the adoption of an ethical standpoint which embraces ecocentrism involves a shift in social and political thought to a new 'politics of obligation'. The prospects for the idea of ecological citizenship are uncertain and current political concerns with rights and entitlements suggest that any attempt to promote a politics of obligation will encounter considerable resistance. Nevertheless, the transformation from an anthropocentric to an ecocentric relationship between society and nature would involve significant shifts in human assumptions, behaviour and institutional structures. Resistance is perhaps inevitable but, given the risks of doing otherwise, we have no free choices left.

References

Bahro, R. (1986) *Building the green movement*. London: Heretic Books.

Barry, B. (1977) 'Justice between generations' in P. M. S. Hacker and J. Raz (eds), *Law, Morality and Society: Essays in Honour of H. L. A. Hart*. Oxford: Clarendon Press.

Beck, U. (1992) *Risk Society: Towards a New Modernity*. London: Sage.

Beck, U. (1995) *Ecological Politics in an Age of Risk*. Cambridge: Polity.

Beck, U., Giddens, A. and Lash, S. (1994) *Reflexive Modernisation: Politics, Tradition and Aesthetics in the Modern Social Order.* Cambridge: Polity.

Benton, T. (1989) 'Marxism and natural limits: an ecological critique and reconstruction', *New Left Review*, 178: 51–87.

Bookchin, M. (1980) *Toward an Ecological Society*. Montreal: Black Rose Books.

Brambell, F. W. R. (1965) *Report of the Technical Committee of Enquiry into the Welfare of Animals Kept Under Intensive Livestock Husbandry Systems,* Cmnd 28. London: HMSO.

Callahan, D. (1971) 'What obligations do we have to future generations?', *American Ecclesiastical Review*, 164 (April): 265–80.

Carson, R. (1962) *Silent Spring*. Harmondsworth: Penguin.

Clark, J. (1989) 'Man's inorganic body', *Environmental Ethics,* 11: 243–58.

Clark, S. L. R. (1977) *The Moral Status of Animals*. Oxford: Clarendon Press.

Collard, A. and Contrucci, J. (1988) *The Rape of the Wild*. London: Women's Press.

Dickens, P. (1992) *Society and Nature: Towards a Green Social Theory*. Hemel Hempstead: Harvester-Wheatsheaf.

Dubos, R. (1980) *The Wooing of the Earth*. London: Athlone Press.

Environmental Action Programme for Central and Eastern Europe (1993)

Document commissioned for the Lucerne Ministerial Conference, Switzerland.

Enzenberger, H. M. (1974) 'A critique of political ecology', *New Left Review*, 84: 3–31.

Frey, R. (1980) *Interests and Rights: The Case against Animals*. Oxford: Clarendon Press.

Giddens, A. (1990) *The Consequences of Modernity*. Cambridge: Polity.

Giddens, A. (1991) *Modernity and Self-Identity*. Cambridge: Polity.

Gittens, D. (1982) *Fair Sex: Family Size and Structure 1900–1939*. London: Hutchinson.

Golding, M. P. (1972) 'Obligations to future generations', *The Monist*, 56: 85–99.

Goldsmith, E. *et al.* (1972) 'A blueprint for survival', *The Ecologist*, 2(1): 1–43.

Gray, J. (1993) *Beyond the New Right: Markets, Government and the Common Environment*. London: Routledge.

Hardin, G. (1993) 'The tragedy of the commons' [1968] in H. Daly (ed.), *Valuing the Earth*. Cambridge, MA: MIT Press.

Harrison, R. (1964) *Animal Machines*. London: Vincent Stuart.

Havel, V. (1988) 'Anti-political politics' in J. Keane (ed.), *Civil Society and the State: New European Perspectives*. London: Verso.

Leopold, A. (1949) *A Sand County Almanac: And Sketches Here and There*. Oxford: Oxford University Press.

Lewis, M. W. (1992) *Green Delusions: An Environmentalist Critique of Radical Environmentalism*. Durham, NC: Duke University Press.

Lukes, S. (1974) *Power: A Radical Approach*. Basingstoke: Macmillan.

Martell, L. (1995) *Ecology and Society: An Introduction*. Cambridge: Polity.

Marx, K. (1977) *Economic and Philosophic Manuscripts of 1844*, revised edn. London: Lawrence and Wishart.

Marx, K. and Engels, F. (1970) *The German Ideology*, ed. C. J. Arthur. London: Lawrence and Wishart. First published in 1845–6.

Meadows, D. H., Meadows, D. L., Randers, J. and Behrens, W. (1972) *The Limits to Growth: A Report for the Club of Rome's Project on the Predicament of Mankind*. London: Pan.

Merchant, C. (1980) *The Death of Nature: Women, Ecology and the Scientific Revolution*. New York: Harper & Row.

Mies, M. and Shiva, V. (1993) *Ecofeminism*. London: Zed Books.

Mills, C. W. (1956) *The Power Elite*. Oxford: Oxford University Press.

Muir, J. (1901) *Our National Parks*. Boston, MA: Houghton Mifflin.

Naess, A. (1973) 'The shallow and the deep, long-range ecology movement: a summary', *Inquiry*, 16: 95–100.

Narveson, J. (1977) 'Animal rights', *Canadian Journal of Philosophy*, vii: 161–78.

Nozick, R. (1974) *Anarchy, State and Utopia.* Oxford: Blackwell.
O'Neill, J. (1993) *Ecology, Policy and Politics: Human Well-Being and the Natural World.* London: Routledge.
Parsons, H. L. (1977) *Marx and Engels on Ecology*. London: Greenwood.
Passmore, J. (1974) *Man's Responsibility for Nature.* London: Duckworth .
Pinchot, G. (1901) *The Fight for Conservation*. New York: Harcourt Brace.
Plant, J. (1989) *Healing the Wounds: The Promise of Ecofeminism.* Philadelphia: New Society.
Plumwood, V. (1990) 'Women, humanity and nature' in S. Sayers and P. Osbourne (eds), *Socialism, Feminism and Philosophy*. London: Routledge.
Rawls, J. (1971) *A Theory of Justice*. Oxford: Oxford University Press.
Regan, T. (1984) *The Case for Animal Rights*. London: Routledge.
Routley, R. and Routley, V. (1978) 'Nuclear energy and obligations to the future', *Inquiry*, 21: 133–79.
Sale, K. (1985) *Dwellers on the Land: The Bioregional Vision*. San Francisco: Sierra Club Books.
Saunders, P. (1995) *Capitalism: A Social Audit.* Buckingham: Open University Press.
Schumacher, F. (1973) *Small is Beautiful: Economics As If People Really Mattered.* London: Abacus.
Seager, J. (1993) *Earth Follies: Feminism, Politics and the Environment.* London: Earthscan.
Singer, P. (1976) *Animal Liberation: Towards an End to Man's Inhumanity to Animals*. Wellingborough: Thorsons.
Singer, P. (1993) *Practical Ethics*, 2nd edition. Cambridge: Cambridge University Press.
Stacey, M. and Price, M. (1981) *Women, Power and Politics*. London: Tavistock.
Stone, C. D. (1972) 'Should trees have standing? – toward legal rights for natural objects', *Southern California Law Review*, 45(2): 450–501.
Stone, C. D. (1987) *Earth and Other Ethics: The Case for Moral Pluralism*. New York: Harper & Row.
Taylor, A. (1992) *Choosing Our Future: A Practical Politics of the Environment.* London: Routledge.
Tester, K. (1991) *Animals and Society: The Humanity of Animal Rights*. London: Routledge.
Thomas, K. (1982) *Man and the Natural World 1500–1800*. Harmondsworth: Penguin.
White Jr, L. (1967) 'The historical roots of our ecological crisis', *Science*, 155: 1203–7.
Yearley, S. (1991) *The Green Case: A Sociology of Environmental Issues, Arguments and Politics*. London: HarperCollins.

Index